EGYPTIAN · BOOKSHELF

BOATS

D1416260

EGYPTIAN · ℬOOKSHELF

BOATS

DILWYN JONES

University of Texas Press
Austin

International Standard Book Number 0-292-74039-5
Library of Congress Catalog Card Number 94-61614
Copyright © 1995 The Trustees of the British Museum

First University of Texas Press edition, 1995
All rights reserved
Printed in Great Britain

Requests for permission to reproduce material from this work
should be sent to Permissions, University of Texas Press,
Box 7819, Austin, Texas 78713-7819.

Designed by Grahame Dudley Associates

Front cover: Wooden model of an Egyptian funerary bark
Frontispiece: Artist's impression of the sailing boat of
Hatshepsut, a sea-going vessel depicted in the funerary
temple at Deir el-Bahri

Contents

Acknowledgements

T his book cannot be anything more than a brief survey of a large and complex subject and the author freely acknowledges his debt to the host of scholars, too many to acknowledge individually, whose works he has consulted during its preparation.

Thanks are due to the following individuals and institutions who have helped me during the preparation of this book: the Griffith Institute Committee for its permission to use material from the Carter Archive; Dr Jaromir Malek and staff of the Topographical Bibliography at the Griffith Institute, Oxford; Mr John Taylor, Librarian of the Griffith Institute Library, Oxford; Mr Harold Parkinson, Mr Mervyn Evans and Mr Gavin Jenkins for the artwork.

I am also grateful to Mr Vivian Davies, The Keeper of the Department of Egyptian Antiquities at the British Museum; Dr Richard Parkinson of the same Department and Dr Yvonne Harpur, Mr Paolo Scremin and Mr Paul Cooper for their help in obtaining photographs; Dr Björn Landström for his kind permission to use illustrations from his book *Ships of the Pharaohs*; Dr David Dixon, the Honorary Secretary of the Egypt Exploration Society; Mr John Larson, Museum Archivist of the Oriental Institute, The University of Chicago; Mr Douglas Champion, for permission to use his drawings and Sandra Shaul, Head of Publication at the Royal Ontario Museum; Celia Clear, Publishing Manager and Carolyn Jones, Editor, of the British Museum Press, for their help in bringing this book to print; and last, but not least, my wife, Cecily, for her encouragement and support during its preparation.

Chronological table

The dates are those cited in J.R. Baines and J. Malek, *Atlas of Ancient Egypt*, Oxford, 1980.

Predynastic Period	
Badarian	
Naqada I	
Naqada II	*c.* 3000 BC
Early Dynastic Period	*c.* 2920–*c.* 2649 BC
(Dynasties I and II)	
Old Kingdom	*c.* 2649–*c.* 2150 BC
Dynasties III–VI)	
First Intermediate Period	*c.* 2150–*c.* 2040 BC
(Dynasties VII–X)	
Middle Kingdom	*c.* 2134–*c.* 1783 BC
(Dynasties XI AND XII)	
Second Intermediate Period	*c.* 1783–*c.* 1550BC
(Dynasties XIII–XVII)	
New Kingdom	*c.* 1550–*c.* 1070 BC
(Dynasties XVIII–XX)	
Late New Kingdom	*c.* 1070–525 BC
(Dynasties XXI–XXVI)	
Late Dynastic Period	525–343 BC
(Dynasties XXVII–XXX)	

Abbreviations

AEL   Lichtheim, M., *Ancient Egyptian Literature*. 3 vols. California, 1973–80.

BAR   Breasted, J.H., *Ancient Records of Egypt*, i–v. Chicago, 1906–7.

FBD   Faulkner, R.O., *The Ancient Egyptian Book of the Dead*. London, 1985.

FCT   Faulkner, R.O., *The Ancient Egyptian Coffin Texts*. 3 vols. London, 1973–8.

FPT   Faulkner, R.O., *The Ancient Egyptian Pyramid Texts translated into English*. Oxford, 1969.

JEA   *The Journal of Egyptian Archaeology*.

KRI   Kitchen, *Ramesside Inscriptions*.

Sp.   Spell (FBD, FCT)

Utt.   Utterance (FPT)

Introduction

'Egypt is the gift of the river'. It was the Greek historian Herodotus (fifth century BC) borrowing the words of an earlier visitor to Egypt who made this now famous comment. This observation remains true today. The Nile, which winds its way northwards for a distance of about 750 miles along the whole length of the country, not only provides Egypt with the famed fertility of its soil, but also offers the swiftest and most convenient means of communication between north and south (see fig. 1, map). The Ancient Egyptians developed two principal types of boats: papyrus skiffs, used locally for hunting and fishing in the marshes; and wooden boats used for longer voyages and for transporting heavy loads. Both types are known to us from tomb paintings and boat-models and from actual wooden boats discovered alongside the royal pyramids at Giza and Dahshur.

No civilisation, ancient or modern, has depended more on water transport for its existence and growth than Egypt. From the earliest period down to modern times, the Nile was the main artery along which commerce and military expeditions moved. Travel by land was always a time-consuming and arduous undertaking in comparison. The movement of men and materials for the building projects and the military expeditions that played such an important role in each successive pharaoh's reign could not have been undertaken without the constant use of water transport. It is not surprising, therefore, that boats were so dominant a feature in the lives of the Ancient Egyptians and so profoundly affected their mental processes and religious thinking. So all pervading was the role of water transport that even the terms for movement north or south were determined by signs that depicted either a boat with its sail raised or one with its mast stowed away. Even technical terms originally used to describe locations aboard a ship, such as starboard and larboard, were employed to denote right and left on land and the Egyptian word for an 'expedition' is illustrated by a kneeling man holding a bow followed by a boat sign.

Nautical metaphors abound. A temple can be said to hold 'the prow-rope of the Southland and the stern-rope of the Northland' (BAR II, §885). Ineni can speak of Queen Hatshepsut as 'the bow-rope of the South, the mooring-stake of the Southerners; the excellent stern-rope of the Northland' (BAR II, §341). Nobles, such as Harkhuf and Nefer-

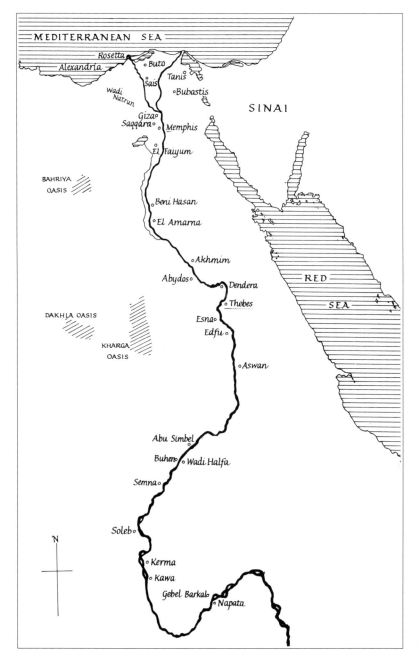

1   *Map of Egypt.*

2 *Drawing of boats on Naqada II pottery.*

sheshemra of the Sixth Dynasty, record in their tomb biographies that, besides giving bread to the hungry and clothes to the naked, they had brought the boatless to land. A similar claim is made by the deceased before the assembled gods in the Hall of Judgement:

> ***I have given bread to the hungry, water to the thirsty, clothes to the naked, a boat to him who was boatless. (FBD, Sp. 125, p. 32)***

Indeed, so closely identified was the ownership of a boat with the means of survival that a certain Wennefer, who lived in the Ptolemaic Period could speak of himself as:

> ***... one who protected the weak from the strong, so as to be a ferryboat for everyone. (AEL III, p. 55)***

From earliest times, the boat was considered indispensable to the deceased's survival in the after-life and was always included among his funerary equipment. Prince Minkhaf, a son of Khufu (Cheops), who served as vizier during the reign of Khafra (2520–2494 BC), had four different types of boats included in a list of offerings carved on the side of his sarcophagus. Kaemankh, who lived during the Sixth Dynasty, not only mentions five different types of boats on the walls of his tomb at Giza, but also shows his whole dockyard, complete with workers and their tools.

The earliest representations of boats are those preserved on decorated predynastic pottery of the Gerzean and Naqada II cultures and in rock-drawings of Upper Egypt and Nubia (fig. 2). Miniature boats made from terracotta, bone and ivory are among some of the earliest objects discovered in Egypt. A large painting of a boating-scene also once decorated the wall of a Late Gerzean tomb discovered at Hieraconpolis, and a boat appears on fragments of a linen cloth from a grave at Gebelein, proving the existence even at this early date of a well-established boat-building tradition. A boat is depicted on the Narmer palette which dates to the period of the unification of Upper and Lower Egypt around 3200 BC and boats appear on ivory and wooden labels from the early dynastic tombs at Saqqara and Abydos.

CHAPTER ONE

Boats in ritual and belief

I n common with many of the world's civilisations, the Ancient Egyptians believed that the dead had to cross a stretch of water, described in the texts as 'the Winding-Waterway', before they could experience resurrection in the hereafter. Travel by boat was a recurrent theme in their religious literature.

> *May the soul of N (the deceased) go up with you to the sky, may he travel in the Day-bark, may he moor in the Night-bark, may he mix with the Unwearying Stars in the sky. (FBD, Sp. 15, p. 41)*

This destination was a place called the 'Fields of Offerings' or the 'Field of Rushes': a fertile land where the deceased could till the soil and live on the rich produce he harvested.

> *The doors of the sky are opened for you, the doors of the firmament are thrown open to you, that you may travel by boat to the Field of Rushes, that you may cultivate barley, that you may reap emmer and prepare your sustenance therefrom like Horus the son of Atum. (FPT, Utt. 461)*

The same thought is expressed much later by the scribe Paheri of El-Kab, who lived under either Tuthmose I or Hatshepsut (1504–1458 BC) of the Eighteenth Dynasty:

> *You cross in the ferry without being hindered. You fare on the water's flowing flood. You come to life a second time.... (AEL II, p. 17)*

It goes without saying, therefore, that the ownership of a boat was considered an essential prerequisite for survival, both in this world and the next, and numerous spells call upon the gods to provide the deceased with the means of passage into the next life:

> *O sounding-poles of Horus, O wings of Thoth, ferry me across, do not leave me boatless. (FPT, Utt. 515)*

> *[Thoth] listens to me; he has removed my impediment, and I will not be boatless, I will not be turned away from the horizon, for I am Ra, I will not be boatless in the great crossing. (FCT III, Sp. 1099)*

Even the king was not immune from such fear:

> *... the ferry-boats are made ready for the son of Atum, for the son of Atum is not boatless. The king is bound for the son of Atum, and the son of Atum is not boatless. (FPT, Utt. 615)*

However, since the majority did not have the means to provide themselves with full-sized boats, they had to make do with miniature copies – models – which would serve as magical substitutes and thereby guarantee them a means of passage into the other world. As the gods and stars traversed the sky and the waters of the Netherworld by boat, so also would the deceased join the sun-god in his bark and cross the sky by day and the river of the Netherworld by night.

The fear of being stranded without a boat gave rise to the so-called *Ferryman Text*. This spell allowed the deceased to summon the 'Ferryman of the Winding-Waterway', appropriately named 'Backwards-Looker' because his face was turned backwards as he poled his boat along, to ferry him across to the other side (pl. I):

> *O Ra commend me to MA-HA.f* [that is, 'Backwards Looker'], *the ferryman of the Winding-Waterway, so that he may bring me his ferry-boat which belongs to the Winding-Waterway, in which he ferries the gods to yonder side of the Winding-Waterway to the eastern side of the sky ... (FPT, Utt. 359)*

However, unlike Charon of Classical times who demanded only an obol as his fee for transporting the dead across the Styx, the Ferryman of the Egyptian after-life was a more fastidious character who could not be bought off so easily. The petitioner had first to demonstrate that he was pure and free from moral blemish:

> *O you who ferry over the righteous boatless as the ferryman of the Field of Rushes, I am deemed righteous in the sky and on earth ... (FPT, Utt. 517)*

that he knew the Ferryman's name and the names of the boat's individual parts (FCT II, Sp. 395, 398; FBD, Sp. 99) and last, but not least, possessed the requisite mental agility – that is, was numerate:

> *May you go aboard the ferry-boat because you know the number of your fingers. (FCT II, Sp. 398)*

Only after the deceased had successfully undergone this crucial interrogation could he expect to be granted permission to enter the ferry-boat and pass from this world into the next.

FUNERARY TEXTS AND UNDERWORLD BOOKS

The *Pyramid Texts* inscribed on the walls of the royal pyramids of the Fifth and Sixth Dynasties and the later *Coffin Texts* painted on the sides of wooden coffins of the Middle Kingdom reveal that, from an early date, the Ancient Egyptians believed that the sun-god, Ra, crossed the sky, at first on two reed floats (*sekhenwey*), later on two papyriform boats – a day-bark (*mandjet*) for his journey across the sky by day and a evening-bark (*mesktet*) for his voyage through the Netherworld (the *Duat*) at night.

Egyptian theologians located the Netherworld at one and the same time within the sky or the body of Nut herself, and below the earth in a place they called the 'Lower Sky'. Through the Netherworld flowed a great tributary of the Nun (the primeval waters which surrounded the world and from which all life emerged) on which the bark of Ra travelled during the hours of night until it re-emerged in the morning in the east.

The so-called 'Books', or compilations of spells, of the New Kingdom, such as *The Book of What-is-in-the-Underworld (Am-Duat)*, *The Book of Gates*, *The Book of Caverns* and *The Books of Day and Night*, continue and develop the same theme. All have their origins in the earlier *Pyramid* and *Coffin* texts and, although each displays its own variation of the sun-god's journey and the process of transformation and regeneration which he had to undergo during his nocturnal voyage, all, in essence, describe Ra's descent into the Netherworld at night in the west and his victorious re-emergence at dawn in the east as Khepri (he who comes into existence) in the form of a scarab beetle.

Equally, the Egyptians could envisage life and death as a part of a perennial cycle where the sky goddess Nut swallowed the bark of the sun in the evening before it passed through her body during the night to re-emerge in the morning between her thighs. This popular concept is graphically illustrated on the alabaster sarcophagus of Sety I (1306–1290 BC) and on the ceiling of Ramses VI's (1151–1143 BC) burial chamber in the Valley of the Kings.

Although the sun-god is often depicted as the sole occupant of the boat, more usually he is accompanied by a retinue of other gods who act as his crew. These usually consist of Wepwawet, the 'Opener-of-the-Ways', Geb, the earth-god, Thoth, the god of writing, Hike and Sia, the personifications of magical power and of cognisance, and Hu, the divine principle of creative speech (fig. 3). Often, Maat, goddess of divine order and justice, is also shown standing on the prow of the sun-bark. As 'Lady of the Bark' it was her role, as her name implied, to guide the bark on its way. In other scenes, different gods take their place in the bark: the hawk-headed Horus, 'the Adorer', Thoth, 'the Bull of Truth', Seth, 'the Vigilant' and another Horus called 'the Guide of the Boat'. On many

3 *Sun boat with its divine crew (from the Book of the Dead of Nu).*

occasions the boat is also said to be manned by the stars:

The King shall go aboard the bark like Ra on the banks of the Winding-Waterway. The King shall be rowed by the Unwearying Stars and shall give orders to the Imperishable Stars ... (FPT, Utt. 697)

Having gained admittance to the bark, the deceased was expected to be an active member of the boat's crew. He had to row and pilot the boat: 'I am he who rows and does not tire in the Bark of Ra' (FCT I, Sps. 159, 161); '...I take my oar, I row Ra when traversing the sky...' (FPT, Utt. 467).

He must also help with the boat's ropes and rigging: 'The bark of Ra travels in the Abyss (that is, the Nun) and it is I who take her bow-rope' (FCT II, Sp. 684); 'I am he who has charge of the rigging in the God's Bark' (FCT I, Sp. 159). He was also expected to supervise the crew: 'I command the god's bark for him' (FPT, Utt. 510) and was allowed to steer the boat: 'N [that is the deceased] is the son of Ra who steers his bark; I will fare upstream at the bow, I will guide the voyages...' (FCT II, Sp. 658).

The deceased often affirms that he has performed his tasks efficiently and boasts that he has helped to drive off the great snake, Apophis, the arch-protagonist of Ra in the Netherworld (FCT II, Sp. 644).

Representations, presumably of the sun-boat, occur on very early Egyptian wooden, ivory and bone labels (fig. 4). These barks are characterised by a sickle-shaped stern and a protective mat or fender draped over the prow. They are equipped with various pieces of deck-furniture whose exact significance is still a matter of conjecture: a board with nine ostrich (*maat*) feathers between two rails, two kinds of standards, sometimes flanked by falcons on poles, and, finally, at least two types of chests. A unique painting of the evening-bark of the sun is to be found on a ceiling of the tomb of Ramses VI of the Twentieth Dynasty: it shows the bark in plan and profile, correctly oriented, sailing eastwards towards the sunrise (fig. 6).

5 *Wooden model of the sun-boat showing deck-furniture.*

A few models of the sun-boat have survived from tombs of the Middle Kingdom notably from Bersheh and Meir, but they are rare (fig. 5). Their purpose lies, as the *Pyramid Texts* tell us, in the deceased's wish to join Ra in his bark. Although originally the exclusive preserve of the dead king,

6 *Painting of the sun boat, on the ceiling of the tomb of Ramses VI from the Valley of the Kings at Thebes.*

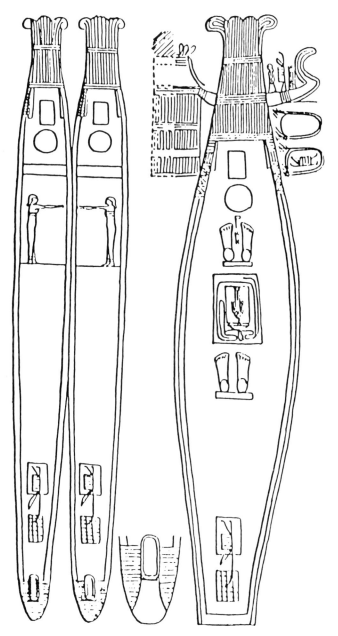

the political and religious upheavals which accompanied the close of the Old Kingdom brought many changes, and it soon became everyone's desire to join Ra after death, with the result that the *Coffin Texts* and the later *Book of the Dead* contain the spell 'For bringing the great bark of Ra' (FBD, Sp. 102 and 136A).

Actual full-sized replicas of the solar-bark stood in all the Heliopolitan sun-temples of the Fifth Dynasty. They were situated outside the temples parallel with their south walls. The 'solar-bark' of king Nyuserra (2416–2392 BC) of the Fifth Dynasty – a 30m imitation of the sun-god's bark

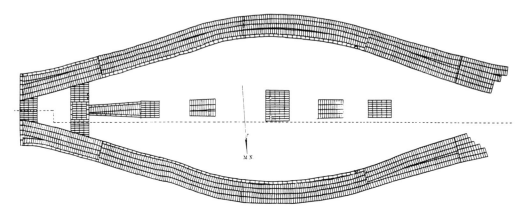

built of mud-brick – was discovered by Ludwig Borchardt in 1900, south of the king's sun-temple at Abu Ghurob near Abusir orientated on a east-west axis, with its prow to the east (fig. 7).

7 *Nyuserra's sunboat, built of mud brick, from his sun-temple at Abu Ghurob.*

FUNERARY JOURNEYS

Tombs from the Middle Kingdom onwards contain two types of scene which depict journeys by water which the deceased made, or was imagined to make, after death.

The first, and most common, depicts a journey (often referred to in modern literature as a 'pilgrimage') which the deceased was believed to make to the sacred sites of Busiris or Abydos, traditionally associated with the god Osiris' birth and death. Although originally worshipped at Busiris, the god's cult soon spread all over Egypt where it eventually became localised at Abydos. From the Middle Kingdom, every pious Egyptian desired to visit Abydos during his lifetime in order to arrange for his burial there or to erect a commemorative chapel on its holy ground, or to participate in the Festival of Osiris celebrated there annually.

Although the majority of Egyptians were buried near their own towns and villages, each sought, after death, to make one last 'pilgrimage' to the holy places in order to ensure the god's favour in the next world. However, because such a 'post-mortem' voyage had by that time probably become more symbolic than real, a scene painted on the tomb wall or wooden models of their mummies on boats had to serve in its place. The scene is nearly always reduced to its essential elements: two funerary boats, carrying either the mummy of the deceased on a bier or the seated statues of the husband and wife, towed either by a sailing-boat or a rowing-boat, representing the journeys to and from the place of pilgrimage. Sometimes, both voyages are conflated into one scene or are painted beside each other in the same register.

The second scene commonly found in tombs depicts the actual crossing of the Nile on the day of burial and the overland journey to the necropolis situated, more often than not, on the west bank (pl. II). Not only was a full-sized funerary boat used to transport the mummy of the deceased across the river but, on reaching the west bank, the coffin was

8 *Men carrying a mummy to his tomb on a boat-shaped bier.*

transferred to a papyriform boat or boat-shaped bier, either actual or miniature, which was dragged on a sledge by men and oxen – in rare cases on a four-wheeled wagon – for its final journey across the desert to the tomb. Actual wooden sledges, which may have been used for this purpose, were discovered south of the pyramid of Senusret I (*c.*1971–1926 BC) at Lisht, and with the Dahshur boats of Senusret III (*c.*1878–1841 BC). The canopy covering the bier was decked with fronds and garlands and figures of the goddesses Isis and Nephthys (Osiris' sisters who, according to myth, reconstituted his body after its dismemberment by his brother Seth), called 'kites', represented either by statuettes or by actual female mourners. In scenes they are often shown standing or kneeling on the boat's fore- and after-decks protecting the coffin with their outstretched arms (fig. 8).

The type of vessel shown in both scenes, 'pilgrimage' and funerary, is always papyriform in shape with either a high vertical finial at the prow and a sickle-shaped finial at the stern ending in stylised papyrus umbels, or two symmetrical shaped finials of the same design decorated with streamers which curve over gracefully inboard. The mummy or seated-statue of the deceased is sheltered under a shrine-shaped canopy amid-ships. The boat is provided with double steering-oars on each quarter and its blades are decorated with stylised lotus flowers and *udjat*-eyes. Often the top of the posts and the butt-ends of the oars are decorated with carved jackal or falconheads (fig. 9). The hull is normally painted green, the colour of resurrection, and is regularly decorated along its sides either

with narrow sheer-lines or a rectangular pattern running parallel with the gunwale. Sacred *udjat*-eyes were also painted on both sides of the prow to protect the vessel and its occupants from harm.

9 *A pair of model steering-oars with jackal-headed finials, from a sacred barge.*

SACRED BARKS

There were two kinds of sacred barks: portable barks, either dragged in procession or borne on the shoulders of priests, and full-sized barks or barges which carried the portable bark-shrines and images of the gods on the Nile, canals or sacred lakes during the celebration of religious festivals (see pp. 22ff.).

Each nome (district) had its own bark housed in a special bark-sanctuary of the principal temple. During major festivals the images of the gods were removed from their shrines and taken in procession around the temple or to visit neighbouring deities. On such occasions the divine image was transported from one location to another in a portable bark-shrine in imitation of the gods who were believed to cross the sky in their magical boats.

When the festival of the local god was celebrated during special times of the year, or when the god or goddess left the precincts of his or her own temple to visit another deity at some other location, the portable barks were carried forth on the shoulders of the temple priests amid great jubilation.

Portable barks containing the cult statues of gods or kings were made in the form of papyriform miniature boats and richly decorated with gold

10 *Portable bark of Amun depicted on the wall-reliefs of the Great Hypostyle Hall at Karnak.*

and precious stones. Their hulls were gilded and their finials at stem and stern were carved in the likeness of the gods or the kings they carried. The stems and sterns were decorated with ornate collars and the shrine containing the image of the god amidships was always partially concealed from profane eyes by a white linen cloth. Although normally housed within their bark-sanctuaries in the temples, they were set on carrying-poles for easy transit from one location to another.

The portable bark of Amun-Ra was carried on five carrying-poles by thirty shaven-headed *waab*-priests, often shown wearing Horus- and Anubis-masks as representatives of the 'Souls' of the ancient cult centres of Pe and Nekhen, in six rows of five. Before and behind the bark walked other priests carrying fans and, on either side, the king and the more senior members of the clergy (fig. 10).

Many individuals boast how they had built such barks. Amenhotep III (1391–1353 BC) tells us that he made a portable bark-shrine called *Amun-has-received-his-divine-bark* for his temple at Thebes 'as a place of rest for the lord of the gods at his Feast of the Valley...' (BAR II, §885).

Similarly, Montuemhat, the 'Prince of Thebes', at the beginning of the Twenty-Sixth Dynasty, informs us that he had adorned or renewed several portable barks – those of Amun-Ra and Mut of Ashru, 'Khons-the-Child' and 'Bastet-residing-in-Thebes', and had 'rebuilt the divine boat of Osiris in Abydos when he found it gone to ruin'.

A sequence of reliefs on the east wall of the processional colonnade in the Temple of Luxor, begun by Amenhotep III and completed during the reign of Tutankhamun, (1333–1323 BC), records in great detail the pomp

and ceremony which surrounded the celebration of the Great Festival of
Ipet. During the festival, the portable barks of Amun, his wife Mut, the
Lady of Asheru, and their child, the moon-god Khons, were carried forth
in procession from the temple in Karnak down to the Nile. There each
was loaded on to his or her own individual full-sized barge. The procession was accompanied on the river and on land by a large throng of
Thebans, contingents of the army, priests and singers. On their arrival at
the temple of Luxor, the portable barks were placed in their individual
sanctuaries. After the completion of the festival, they were taken back by
river to their respective temples at Karnak.

    Much later, during the reign of Ptolemy VIII (170–163, 145–116 BC), a
similar scene in the temple of Edfu records the arrival of a flotilla of seven
boats bringing the portable bark of the goddess Hathor of Dendera on
her annual visit to the temple for the celebration of the 'Festival of the
Perfect Reunion' or sacred marriage to Horus.

    Perhaps the two portable barks most often mentioned in our sources
are the 'Henu-bark' of Sokar (fig. 11) and the 'Neshmet-bark' of Osiris,
which were used to transport the cult images of the gods during religious
ceremonies held annually at Memphis and Abydos.

*11 Sacred bark of Sokar
with an antelope's head at
the prow. A vignette from
the papyrus of Ani.*

Userhat

The *Userhat* (perhaps, 'Powerful-of-Prow'), or the 'Great Barge of the
Head-of-the-River', as it was sometimes called, was the sacred river barge

12 *The Userhet, the ceremonial barge of the god Amun, depicted on the wall reliefs of the Great Hypostyle Hall at Karnak.*

13 *Ram's head finial from the sacred barge of Amun.*

par excellence. It was used at Thebes during religious festivals as a virtual floating temple to convey the portable bark of Amun-Ra, the king of the gods, from his cult centre at Karnak to other sacred locations during the 'Festival of Ipet' and the 'Beautiful Festival of the Valley', (pl. III, fig. 12). During such festivals it was towed in procession by other boats down the Nile to the temple of Luxor, or along a canal that once linked the Nile with the west bank to visit the mortuary temples which were located there. The survival of several scenes portraying the barge has allowed scholars to reconstruct its appearance in some detail and, although the composition of the symbols and number of its crew vary over the years, its characteristic features remain remarkably consistent.

The bow and stern finials were carved in the shape of rams' heads with *uraei* on their brows wearing *atef*-crowns surmounted by solar disks above and decked with broad collars below (fig. 13). On the fore-deck stood a falcon on a pole crowned with the solar disk and double feathers. Immediately behind it on the larboard and starboard sides stood images of the goddesses Maat and Hathor and a royal sphinx on a standard.

Four tall, slender columns with lotus-bud capitals surmounted by the reigning king's cartouches and falcons with solar disks and double-feathered crowns stood amidships before the bark-shrine. Immediately to their rear stood two tall obelisks, sheathed in gold and, behind these, two flagpoles decked with streamers. Sometimes a group of kneeling spirits, representing the 'Souls' of Pe and Nekhen, was shown doing homage to the central naos containing the portable bark-shrine of Amun.

The portable bark itself rested within a magnificent shrine amidships under a richly-decorated baldachin supported on slender columns (fig. 14). The shrine, earlier veiled but later shown open, had a cornice and a frieze of *uraei*, and its side-panelling was decorated with royal cartouches, *uraei*, *djed* pillars and *tyet* amulets.

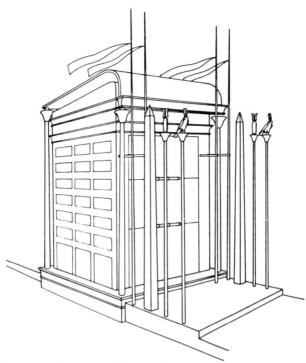

14   *Golden shrine on the bark of Amun.*

The huge vessel was steered by two large steering-oars suspended over each quarter. The butt-ends of the steering-oars, and the posts supporting them, were surmounted by rams' heads (fig. 15). The whole length of the hull on either side was covered in gold leaf and decorated with panels depicting the king and the gods performing various religious ceremonies.

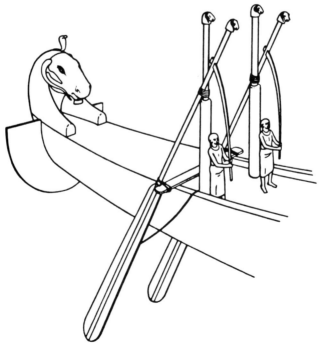

15   *Double steering oars on the bark of Amun.*

16 *Wooden model of the sacred bark of Amun.*

There is a crudely-carved wooden model of the sacred bark of Amun with rams' head finials in the British Museum. Its shrine amidships and other insignia have long disappeared, but it was once painted yellow to imitate the gold leaf which once covered the actual portable bark of Amun-Ra (fig. 16).

Many kings and high officials of state recount how they had either refurbished the barge or built a new one. Ahmose, the founder of the Eighteenth Dynasty, tells us, in what is possibly the earliest extant textual reference to the barge, that he built 'a barge of the "Beginning-of-the-River" named *Userhat* of new cedar of the best of the terraces' (BAR II, §32).

Amenhotep III has left us the most complete description of the vessel on his great stela from his mortuary temple in western Thebes:

> *I made another monument for my father Amun-Ra Lord of Thrones-of-the-Two-Lands, who set me on his throne, in making for him a great bark upon the river,* **Amun-Ra-firm-of-brow,** *of new pine wood cut by my majesty in the countries of god's land and dragged from the mountains of Retjenu by the chiefs of all foreign lands. It is very wide and great; the like has never been made. Its interior is made pure with silver; it is worked with gold throughout. A great shrine of fine gold fills the entire surface. Its projecting ends double [its] length and bear great* atef-crowns. *Their uraeus-serpents coiled about their sides, provide their protection. Before it stand flagpoles worked with fine gold, and two tall great obelisks are between them. It is beautiful on all sides . . . (BAR II, §888; AEL II, p. 45)*

Some indication of the enormous amount of wealth that was lavished on its decoration is given by another inscription in the temple of Ramses III:

> *Electron: 50,000 deben; silver: 4000 deben; black copper: 2000 deben; pure copper: 300,000 deben; lapis lazuli: 3600 deben; malachite: 6600 deben; precious stones: 3300 deben.*
> *(1 deben = 91 grammes; KRI V, 3, p.187, 16ff)*

CHAPTER TWO

Sources
of evidence

A part from tomb paintings and temple reliefs, which are by far the most common source of information, our knowledge of Ancient Egyptian shipping is derived from tomb models and actual boats which have survived the ravages of time, such as the Khufu boat and the boats discovered buried alongside the pyramid of Senusret III (c.1878–1841 BC) at Dahshur (see pp. 76–80).

Since tomb paintings and temple reliefs are referred to throughout, this section will concentrate on the physical evidence provided from other sources.

BOAT MODELS

The dead were believed to need the use of several boats, both actual and divine, in the next life, just as they did other domestic objects. Each boat had its own specific name, shape and function. Several small wooden, ivory and clay boats (fig. 17) have survived from the early period, but it is unclear whether these miniatures can be classed as models for the use of the deceased in the after-life or as children's playthings.

Model boats first became a regular part of burial equipment in the Sixth Dynasty. Usually at least two boats were included in the burial, correctly oriented: one rigged with a sail for voyaging upstream, and another with its mast unstepped and stowed away on the deckhouse roof for rowing downstream. However, these miniature boats are not models as we would understand the term today, but objects endowed with magical power which enabled the deceased to journey from this life to the next and to be independent of the favours of the celestial Ferryman (see previous chapter).

Although boat models occur in such diverse materials as pottery, bone, metal and ivory, the vast majority, apart from a unique model buried

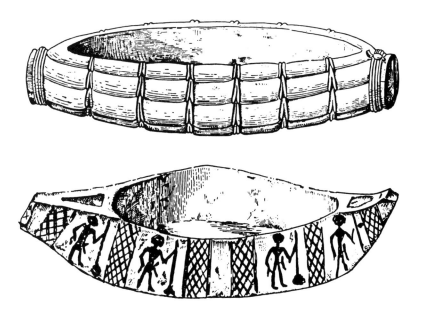

near the mastaba of Imhotep at Lisht, which was built in the same way and with precisely the same number of planks as a full-sized boat, are normally carved and shaped from a single solid block of wood. The finials at the bow and stern and the deckhouse, look-out platforms, mast and rigging are made from separate pieces of wood and pegged on to the main body of the hull. Normally, the whole hull is coated with a thin layer of gesso (white plaster) and painted. On early models the internal structure of the boat is shown in miniature. Later, however, different parts of the boat are represented schematically by different paint colours: red and yellow for the planking and beam work, white for movable deck hatches and black for ties of leather and cord.

On the basis of function, the models fall into three main categories: boats which it was believed would be needed by the deceased in the after-life for travelling, carrying freight, hunting or pleasure; boats used for funerary purposes to transport the mummy of the deceased across the Nile or to take him on journeys to Abydos or to other sacred sites; and lastly, magical boats (usually confined to royalty, although a few examples occur in private tombs) for the use of the king in a solar hereafter to cross the sky by day and the underworld by night. These magical boats must not be confused with the funerary or passenger boats whose sole purpose it was to provide the deceased with a similar means of transport in the after-life as he had enjoyed on earth.

Apart from a few small figures of rowers and some models of boats found in the tombs of the Fifth and Sixth Dynasty, the first large collection of model boats, eight in number, which has survived was found in the tomb of the Nomarch, Niankh-Pepy-Kem at Meir, dating to the time of Pepy II (2246–2152 BC). All are shaped from solid blocks of wood with separately carved fixtures such as masts, oars and stanchions. Some are flat bottomed with projecting platforms at the stern and equipped with the only small-scale models of bipod masts that have survived from the period, while others are round bottomed and spoon shaped and equipped with pole masts (fig. 18).

A further sixteen models were discovered by Gustav Jéquier in a large pit beside the pyramid of Queen Neith (wife of Pepy II) at Saqqara. The hulls were fashioned as before from solid blocks of wood with the superstructures and the more delicate pieces carved from separate pieces of wood and fitted to the hull with pegs or mortise-and-tenon joints. Each boat was provided with its own equipment: large steering-oars with flat projecting tillers, rowing oars or paddles with lancet shaped blades, landing planks, bailors, mallets and mooring stakes. Jéquier believed that the boats were abandoned probably after serving their purpose of magically transporting the deceased's mummy and cortège across the Nile (figs 19, 20).

The last large group which has survived from the Old Kingdom was discovered at the mouth of a Sixth Dynasty burial shaft of the mastaba of Kaemsenu. It consisted of eleven small, crudely-carved, wooden model boats equipped with oars, bipod masts, and other accessories (fig. 21).

By far the largest number of model boats held in today's museum

18 *(Left) Model boats of Ni-ankh-Pepy-Kem ('the Black').*

19 *(Right) Model boats of Queen Neith.*

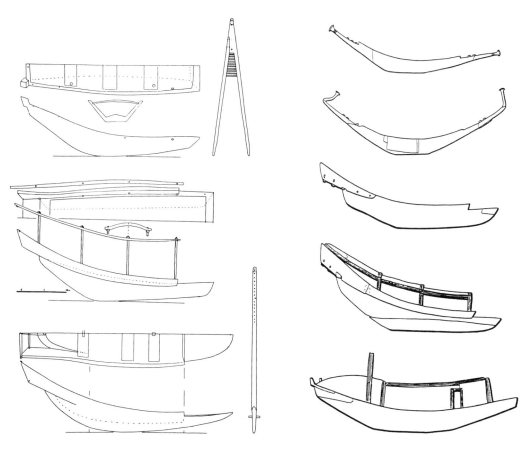

20 *Artist's impression of one of Queen Neith's travelling boats.*

21 *Model boats from Kaemsenu's tomb at Saqqara.*

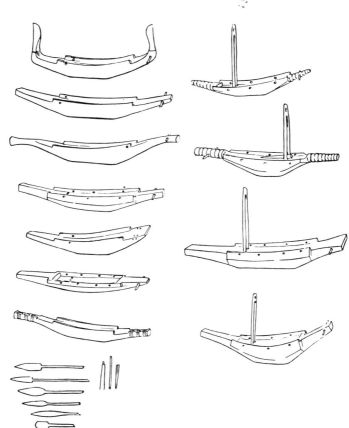

collections come from the Middle Kingdom, and none is finer than the one which belonged to Meketra, the Chancellor of King Nebhepetra Mentuhotep II (2061–2010 BC). These were discovered in March 1920 by H.E. Winlock in a tomb a little to the south of the temple of Mentuhotep at Deir el-Bahari. The flotilla consists of four travelling-boats: two under sail, two rowed; two kitchen tenders; four papyriform craft of similar type to the Khufu boat; two sporting-boats to supply the deceased with fish and fowl; and, finally, two light papyrus skiffs with a trawl slung between them (figs. 22–26).

Only two model boats are known from the period between the Middle and New Kingdoms but, in contrast to most, one is made of gold and the other of silver. Both were found in the tomb of Ahmose's (1552–1527 BC) mother, Queen Ahhotep (fig. 27). The gold model is papyriform in shape with stylised papyrus umbels at bow and stern and is about 4.3 m in length. It is rowed by twelve men, sitting alongside the gunwales on either side, and is steered by one large steering-oar at the stern. There are

22–26 *Five model boats from the tomb of Meketra at Thebes.*

22 *Papyriform boat, with crew raising a (now non-existent) sail.*

23 *Sporting boat.*

24 *Travelling boat.*

25 *Travelling boat.*

26 *Papyrus skiffs with a trawl-net between them.*

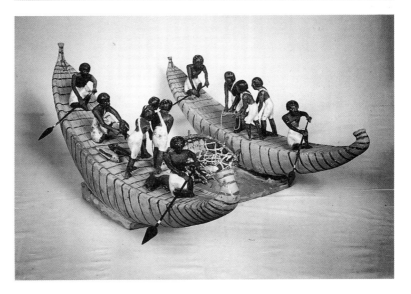

look-out platforms on the fore- and after-decks. The whole vessel is supported on a four-wheeled wagon. Similar wagons are shown in a painting from the tomb of Sobeknakht of the Second Intermediate Period at El-Kab and in a later scene from the tomb of Petosiris dating to the third century BC. The silver model is also papyriform in shape and is paddled by ten men, five on either side.

27   *Golden model of a boat on a four-wheeled wagon, from the tomb of Ahhotep, the mother of Ahmose.*

Although a few damaged models and parts of models had already been found in the tombs of Amenhotep II and Tuthmose III, the only complete flotilla to have survived from the Eighteenth Dynasty was discovered by Howard Carter in 1922 at Thebes in the Tomb of Tutankhamun. Tutankhamun's fleet consisted of thirty-five models – the largest ever found – and provided scholars with the only complete collection of boat models that has survived from this period (see Appendix I).

Although the models show a clear development in design from the earlier boat types found in Meketra's tomb, their actual method of construction differs little from that of their predecessors. Each is sculpted from a solid block of wood with accessories – mast, yards, deckhouse and

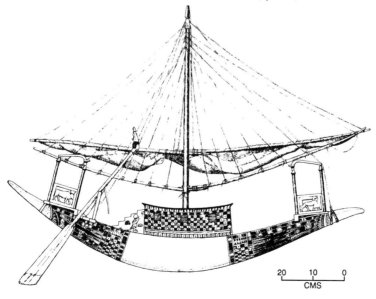

28   *Wooden model of a travelling boat from the tomb of Tutankhamun.*

20   10   0

CMS

32

so on – carved, as before, from separate pieces of wood and glued or pegged on to the main body of the model. The flotilla is divided broadly into two main types: boats which represent actual vessels used on the Nile, and those which represent craft of a more ritual nature.

The first group contains twelve small sailing-boats, each with a single mast and a single steering-oar; four vessels with a deckhouse amidships and a single steering-oar, two of which also had decorated kiosks on their fore-decks and eight boats with two-tiered deckhouses amidships and double steering-oars. Finally, there were three large, fully-rigged vessels with highly decorated baldachins at stem and stern, single-roofed deck-houses amidships and double steering-oars (fig. 28).

The boats of the second type include two which were decorated to represent reed-floats with ends painted to simulate papyrus bundles; two of the type generally described as funerary barks with stems and sterns terminating in papyrus umbels which curve inwards towards their centres; and, finally, four of the solar-bark type with vertical prows and sickle-shaped finials at their sterns. These boats have cuboid thrones amidships similar to those shown on tomb walls and in the vignettes of funerary papyri. Except for the skiffs, which would have been poled or paddled, all these models were equipped with double steering-oars at the stern (fig. 29).

29 *(Top) Celestial ferry-boat or solar boat and (below) funerary or pilgrimage boat from the tomb of Tutankhamun.*

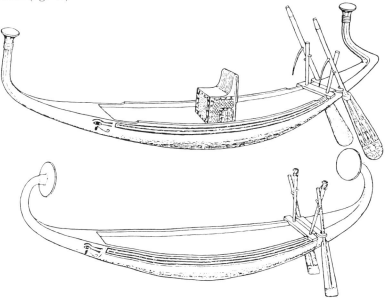

BOAT PITS

Until the discovery of the First Dynasty tombs at Saqqara, the practice of interring full-sized boats alongside tombs was believed to have begun in the Fourth Dynasty and to have been confined to members of the royal family. However, when Emery discovered a brick grave containing a wooden bark north of the mastaba of King Aha at Saqqara and others at the same site (fig. 30), scholars quickly realised that the practice had its origins in a far more remote era. The subsequent discovery by Zaki Saad of nineteen graves for wooden barks buried near individual tombs at Helwan confirmed that the practice was not the sole preserve of royalty, but was also the custom among members of the upper classes. The poorer classes, who could not afford full-sized boats, had to content themselves with models.

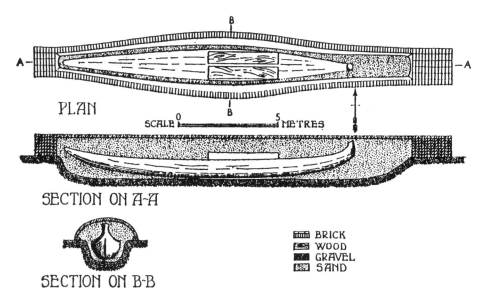

PLAN

SCALE 0 5 METRES

SECTION ON A-A

SECTION ON B-B

▓ BRICK
▓ WOOD
▓ GRAVEL
▓ SAND

Khufu (2551–2528 BC) had five boat pits excavated around his pyramid at Giza. Two lie along its east face, north and south of the mortuary temple. Another is aligned with the causeway and a further two lie along its southern side – one of which has been opened while the other remains sealed with limestone blocks. The remains of another pit was discovered by Chassinat near the pyramid of Radjedef (2528–2520 BC) further north at Abu Roash.

30 *Reconstruction of the boat-pit of Aha.*

Four large rock-cut boat pits were also discovered to the north and south of Khafra's (2520–2494 BC) mortuary temple as well as another along the east face of his pyramid. A deep cleft in the rock running north–south probably represents a sixth vessel. A boat-hieroglyph discovered at Menkaura's (2490–2472 BC) pyramid may indicate the presence of at least one boat-pit in its vicinity. Later, at the end of the Fifth Dynasty, Unas (2356–2323 BC) had a boat pit excavated next to his causeway at Saqqara. Its discoverer tells us that 'it was cut into the rock and cased with white limestone masonry laid in sloping lines to imitate the shape of a wooden hull'. What may be the groove of a second boat was found in 1949 parallel with the one situated on the south side. Apart from the boats of Senusret III of the Twelfth Dynasty, the practice seems to have died out after the close of the Old Kingdom, probably because the custom of burying full-sized boats had become too costly and models could just as readily serve the same purpose.

Royal wives seem also to have been provided with boats. Merytyetes, Khufu's principal queen and the daughter of Sneferu (2575–2551 BC), had a boat pit on the south side of her pyramid at Giza (GIa of Reisner), and Queen Khentkawes, the wife of Userkaf (2465–2458 BC), was similarly provided with a boat pit in the south-west corner of her grave near the Sphinx at Giza.

Although such burials are unusual in private tombs of the period, curious boat-shaped double rooms with curving walls were discovered at Abusir in the south-west corner of the mastaba of Ptahshepses, a high official and a relative of King Nyuserra (2416–2392 BC) of the Fifth Dynasty. Whether these were meant to house imitations of the morning and evening barks of the sun or the actual boats used to convey his body to the tomb is not known. Two long, narrow chambers were also found on top of the mastaba of Kagemni at Saqqara, a vizier under King Teti (2323–2291 BC) of the Sixth Dynasty. These measured 11m in length and 2m in breadth in the middle and tapered towards their ends. Although apparently undisturbed and empty when found, the excavators thought that 'from their shape, the rooms were built to contain or imitate solar-barques'.

The reason why the Ancient Egyptians buried boats close to their tombs has long been the subject of scholarly debate. It has been suggested that there may have been two different traditions underlying the practice. Those pits located to the north of graves in the Early Dynastic Period, may reflect a belief in a stellar hereafter which envisaged the dead king's journey to the stars, while later groups of pits, which were located on several sides of pyramids, may be connected with the belief in a solar hereafter and the dead king's journey in company with the sun-god aboard his two barks. It has been suggested that the Khufu boat may, therefore, be a copy of the *mandjet* or morning-bark, while the un-excavated boat still lying in the other pit may contain the representation of the *mesktet* or evening-bark (see p. 14). However, the Khufu boat does not display any of the characteristic attributes usually associated with the pictorial representations of the solar-bark, and Ahmed Youssef Moustafa, who was responsible for restoring the boat to its original state, was of the opinion that the vessel was probably a funerary boat used to transport the king's body across the Nile to its final resting place on the Giza Plateau – a view supported by rope marks on the boat's wood caused by shrinkage on contact with water.

More recently 'a virtual fleet' of twelve wooden boats encased in brick-built boxes has been discovered at Abydos arranged in a row near the north corner of King Khasekhemwy's funerary enclosure dating, perhaps, to the reign of Djer (First Dynasty). This is a significant discovery which it is hoped will provide us with more information on boat burials and boat-building techniques in Ancient Egypt.

CHAPTER THREE

Ancient Egyptian boats

T his chapter will examine the different types of boats used by the Ancient Egyptians, their functions, and the technical improvements which were introduced to improve their performance during the period under review.

OLD KINGDOM
In the Old Kingdom, apart from papyrus skiffs which were used locally to carry light loads and for fishing and fowling in the marshes (see below), there were four classes of vessels.

River vessels
The hulls of river craft were either cut off square at the bow and stern or ended at the prow in a carved animal figure-head, possibly that of a hedgehog or calf. They were built with edge-joined planks with internal bracing (see pp. 76ff.) and were generally flat bottomed with angular bilges terminating in flat transoms fore and aft. Scenes show that they were trimmed so that the stern was a little higher than the bow, while the midships section was practically horizontal.

Unlike sea-going vessels, (see below) there were no rope-trusses, but what may be called a washstrake or a movable upper strake was attached to the gunwales to keep out spray which extended within a short distance of the extreme bow and stern. The deck was partially removable since the crew are often shown on a lower level than the passengers with their heads protruding above the upper edge of the gunwale. Quarters for the crew were provided for by a small shelter abaft the mast consisting either of a simple awning slung over four or more slender posts, or a more substantial structure covered with plaited matting. This, it seems, was

31 *Old Kingdom sailing boat from the tomb of Kaemankh at Giza.*

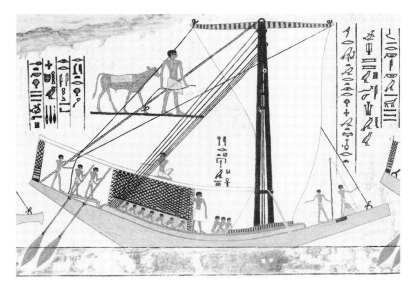

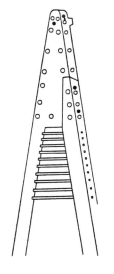

32 *Bipod mast.*

strong enough to support the weight of a crew member who is often shown sitting on top of it giving instructions to the helmsmen (fig. 31).

River vessels were equipped with bipod- or straddle-masts stepped well forward. This type of mast may originally have been devised to spread its load on lighter papyrus craft. Despite its size, however, it could be unstepped when not in use and stowed away on forked crutches. One leg was rebated into the other at the head to assure a good join and the whole structure was further strengthened at intervals by several cross-pieces (fig. 32). The mast-head often ended in a curve or had a square stop-pin, which were probably intended to provide a secure seating for the upper yard when in place. Sometimes it ended in a ring through which the halyard ran.

In the Fourth Dynasty the mast was secured to the stern with a back-stay attached to the mast-head and made fast to rope-loops in the deck planking, but by the Fifth Dynasty a fore-stay was added to give it extra stability. There do not appear to have been any shrouds, but some of the numerous back-stays which are conventionally shown leading back at a slant from the mast-head to the stern of the boat may, in real life, have been attached to the deck or gunwales on either side of the mast to provide it with athwartship support.

Although no actual evidence has survived, when stepped, the legs of the mast most probably fitted into sockets cut into wooden blocks or frames on the hull bottom, while the whole structure was kept firmly in place by trusses under tension lashed, at one end, to one of its cross-pieces and, at the other, to a cross-beam in the deck. Many Old Kingdom scenes show such trusses stretched obliquely between the mast-legs.

The sail was tall and narrow and tapered a little towards its foot. It was bent to two yards and extended from the mast-head to the level of the deck planking. The boom or lower yard rested on the deck abaft the mast.

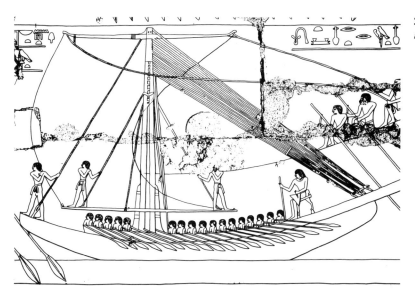

On primitive craft, the sail may, originally, have been made of papyrus matting, but this material probably proved too flimsy and was quickly replaced by linen. The sail was attached to the upper yard either directly or, later, by a kind of saddle-piece and was hoisted to the mast-head by a halyard which passed either through a simple hole or a ring at the mast-head. The halyard was then brought down between the mast-legs and secured either to one of the cross-pieces on the lower-half of the mast or to a rope-loop in the deck. From the Fifth Dynasty there were often two halyards which eased the work load of the crew.

The sail stitching was always horizontal and not vertical as in later times, and its fabric was dyed with various colours. Although never shown in Old Kingdom scenes, the sail leeches probably had bolt-ropes to prevent them from fraying. The sail was attached to the yards by a rope which passed around the yard and into eyelets pierced in the bolt-ropes. Once hoisted, the sail was trimmed to take full advantage of the wind by a pair of braces which were attached to the outer extremities of the upper yard. Sheets for controlling the lower yard were not introduced until a later date when the boom was carried much higher above deck.

Evidence for the existence of bowlines to keep the leading edge of the sail flat when sailing on the wind is provided by a rare scene from the tomb of Seshemnefer (early Fifth Dynasty) at Giza which shows sailors hauling on ropes attached to the leeches of the sail at mid-point (fig. 34).

Old Kingdom boats were steered by one or more hand-held steering-oars suspended over the quarters. The looms of the oars were either worked in rope or leather grommets, or supported in semi-circular grooves cut into the ends of a cross-beam inset into the deck immediately forward of them. The oars were operated either by turning them on their axes or by levering them against the boat's side so that the boat turned in the direction of the blade's outward thrust.

34 *Bowlines are clearly shown on this boat from the tomb of Seshemnefer.*

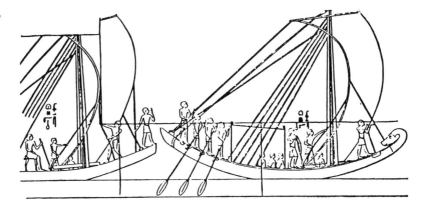

34 *Bowlines are clearly shown on this boat from the tomb of Seshemnefer.*

Equipment was of the simplest kind and consisted of mooring-stones in the form of truncated triangles with holes or grooves at their tops, gangplanks and fenders of wickerwork (see p. 69).

It was probably not until the beginning of the Sixth Dynasty that any significant changes occurred to the rigging and the sail. Five sailing-ships are depicted in the tomb of Mereruka, the vizier of Pepy I (2289–2255 BC), three equipped with bipod masts and two with pole-masts. The sails were no longer tall and narrow but rectangular in shape and were carried higher above the deck. Because of the increase in the sail's size and its height above deck, the yards had to be suspended in lifts. The rope-trusses which supported the mast on earlier vessels were replaced by two stout vertical stanchions lashed to the mast on either side. No sheets are shown, but these must have existed to control the angle of the boom which no longer rested on the deck. The steering-oars were fitted with short cross-pieces near their butt-ends to give the steersman better control, but no attempt was made, as yet, to mount the oar on a vertical stanchion (fig. 33).

Similar changes are depicted in a damaged painting of a river-boat from the Theban tomb of the 'Overseer of Upper Egypt', Unas-Ankh, dating perhaps, to the end of the Fifth or beginning of the Sixth Dynasty. As far as can be discerned, the hull retained its traditional shape. It was square ended and the deck was extended at the stern by means of a strake above the gunwale which projected platform-like beyond the end of the hull. The vessel appears to ride a little higher in the water than previously, but the details are unclear. It was equipped with a pole mast and a wide sail carried high above the deck. The mast was supported by fore- and back-stays. Both yards were hung in topping-lifts and the sail was hoisted by a halyard which descended to the deck immediately abaft the mast. The boat had two cabins, one at the extreme stern and another immediately forward of it decorated with a chequer pattern. The boat was steered by a single long oar which was, perhaps, secured to an upright stanchion(?). The sail-stitching was horizontal and its fabric was decorated with a zigzag-like pattern (fig. 35).

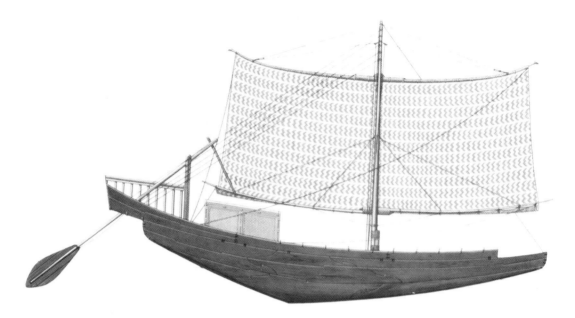

Paintings from Sixth Dynasty tombs at Deir el-Gebrawi and Meir show hulls with bottoms which break at an angle aft of midships, perhaps, as has been suggested, to allow rapid trimming fore and aft permitting them to sail with a wind that was not directly astern. As with the Unas-Ankh boat, there was a projecting platform at the stern and the boats seem to ride higher in the water than before. The low, broad sail on these ships may also indicate an attempt to sail closer to the wind. A powerful forked knee supported the mast, and the single steering-oar, equipped with a long tiller, was mounted perhaps, as has been suggested, on a cable stretched between two poles in the projecting stern.

35 *Unas-Ankh's sailing boat, late Old Kingdom.*

Sea-going vessels

Although sea-going boats shared much in common with their riverine counterparts, there is sufficient difference in detail to treat them under a separate heading.

The type is well represented in a series of reliefs from the mortuary temple of Sahura (2458–2446 BC) of the Fifth Dynasty, which show the departure and subsequent return of a fleet of twelve large ships (pl. IV). Their hulls were long and slender and, in contrast to river boats of the same period, ended in upright knife-shaped finials which provided them with extra protection while at sea. They were probably built in the same manner as their riverine counterparts, that is, with edge-joined planks with internal bracing. They had no keel, so in order to strengthen the hull for sea voyages, shipwrights had invented two new features. The first was a hogging-truss – a heavy rope which was attached to a cross-beam in the bows and then carried aft along the length of the deck on several forked stanchions and made fast to another cross-beam situated below the

36 *Hogging-truss on one
of Sahura's boats.*

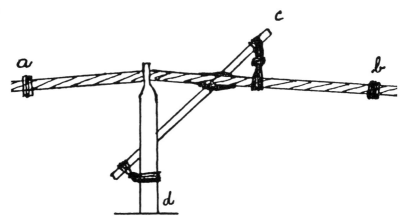

after-deck. A lever thrust between the strands enabled the crew to twist
the rope like a tourniquet and apply the necessary tension to keep the
overhanging bow and stern from sagging. Without the truss, the 'hogging' (pitching) caused by the waves could have broken the ship's back.

The way in which the hogging-truss worked is clearly visible in the
reliefs (fig. 37) and little can be added to Faulkner's description of the
apparatus (see fig. 36): a lever (**c**) was thrust through the strands and
turned until the truss acquired the requisite degree of tautness. Seizings
on the truss at (**a**) and (**b**) and elsewhere along its length, helped localise
the effect of the twisting so that the truss turned as a solid whole. When
the required degree of tautness had been achieved, one end of the lever
was lashed to the truss itself while the other end was secured to the
midships crutch.

37 *Relief of Sahura's
boat showing the hogging
truss in use.*

The second new feature was a narrow girdle-truss that encircled the upper part of the hull at deck level, just below the gunwale. This probably served to prevent the planking there from starting under the pressure exerted by the deck-beams. Short vertical strips of similar lacing linked the main girdle and the gunwale, and probably helped to keep it securely in place and prevent it from slipping down the hull. There were also strips at the extreme bow and stern which joined the main girdle. This network of intersecting ropes worked together to provide additional support to the hull in the absence of a keel and to take the pressures exerted on it by the upward pull of the hogging-truss.

The boats probably had short half-decks fore and aft. The after-deck was railed-in to provide protection for the captain and the helmsman, while the fore-deck was used probably only by the 'pilot' for manoeuvering in shallow waters or when mooring.

As with river boats, the rig consisted of a bipod mast stepped forward of amidships which was equipped with a tall, narrow sail which could be unstepped when required and lowered, as on river boats, on to forked stanchions or, as in this case, on to a gantry at the stern. Comparison with river vessels would suggest that the mast would have been held in place by fore- and after-stays and by tackles of twisted rope under heavy tension at its foot to prevent it from lifting under the pressure of the wind. Shrouds may also have been attached to the ends of the cross-pieces on the mast to provide it with extra athwartship support. Although all the masts on the Sahura boats are unstepped, it must be assumed that the shape of the sails and the rigging would not have differed substantially from those in use on river vessels.

In order to present the maximum effective surface to the wind, two forked spars for extending the leeches of the sail were employed, one on either side of the sail. Their butts were secured to the deck, probably near the foot of the mast, while their forked ends were inserted into eyelets in its leeches. An identical spar, similarly located in the prow of a boat, is depicted on a fragment of an Old Kingdom relief now in the collection of University College, London. On the Sahura boats these spars can be seen lying in the bows. The ships were steered by three large, hand-held oars on either quarter. Each oar was secured by a guard-rope wound around its loom, just above the blade, and attached to the gunwale.

Cargo boats

The hulls of cargo boats either tapered slightly towards the bows or were cut off square, ending in bulkheads. They rode much lower in the water and were much broader in the beam (pl. V). They were often fitted with girdle-trusses to help strengthen the hull planking. The midships area was either left free for cargo or was occupied by a large, roughly rectangular structure apparently made of interwoven lattice-work within which grain or livestock could be carried. This structure was either left open to the sky or had a solid, flat or convex roof with a doorway usually about half-way along its longer side. The cargo was put in this house and on its roof and sometimes below deck in the hull, although more often than not it was shown carried on deck where the cross-beams could support its weight. Livestock was sometimes carried on the forward deck. A small shelter for the crew with its roof curving down to deck level occupied the stern of the vessel.

The steering gear was similar to that on passenger boats and consisted either of hand-held oars secured to the gunwales by a rope or leather grommets, or of a steering-oar on each quarter lashed to a stanchion fixed on the gunwales. The oars were controlled by tillers which sloped forwards so that one person could handle both.

The tomb of Mereruka, dating to the Sixth Dynasty, preserves a fragmentary picture of a cargo boat under sail. More often, the bipod mast was unstepped and was shown with its yards and rigging stowed on top of the deckhouse roof (fig. 38).

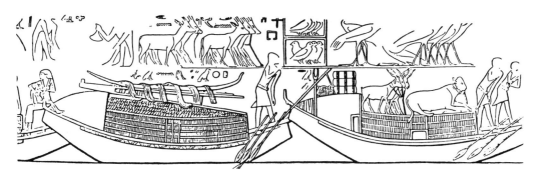

38 *Cargo boat with mast and rigging on its roof, from the tomb of Kagemni at Saqqara.*

Oars were used when travelling downstream. The oarsmen sat on benches behind a low railing near the bows or stood with one foot on the railing for better leverage.

The simpler cargo boats of this class were much smaller and had nothing on deck except supports to carry the mast and rigging. They are sometimes shown being towed in convoy.

Papyriform boats

The fourth class of vessel used in the Old Kingdom was the papyriform boat – a wooden copy of the double-ended papyrus boat made of papyrus-reed bundles. Papyriform boats were used for ceremonial and religious purposes and as a means of transporting the deceased and the grave goods across the river to the necropolis (fig. 39).

At each end was a wooden imitation of a projecting single bundle of papyrus with lashings round it at frequent intervals. These end bundles were flattened out on top like the rest of the deck and it had a bipod mast and tabernacle. There was a shelter at the stern and the double steering-oars were supported against a cross-beam. These papyriform boats were

usually paddled, although a painting from the chapel of Akhethotep-hery of the Fifth Dynasty, now in Leiden, shows one under oar.

39 *Wooden model of Old Kingdom papyriform boat.*

Papyrus skiffs
Mention must also be made here of what was probably the oldest and most common forms of transport in Egypt: the humble papyrus skiff. These craft were used by the earliest inhabitants for local traffic and for hunting and fishing in the marshes.

In comparison with wood, which was always a precious commodity in Egypt, papyrus was plentiful and easily worked. When worn with use, papyrus skiffs could be easily discarded and replaced by new ones. Because of their religious significance, such craft continued to be depicted in tomb scenes even though, one suspects, they had fallen out of general use among the richer classes. Tomb paintings of the Old Kingdom and Middle Kingdoms show the harvesting and transport of papyrus and its use in the manufacture of papyrus skiffs (fig. 40), and nobles constantly depict themselves hunting and spearing fish from such craft. A pair of statuettes from the tomb of Tutankhamun show the boy king himself, harpoon in hand, standing on similar skiffs.

The manufacture of papyrus skiffs was an ancient skill and intimately connected with Egyptians' beliefs in the after-life. Several Utterances in the *Pyramid Texts* describe the 'double reed floats' (*sekhenwey*) on which the king was believed to cross the sky in the company of the sun-god, Ra (see pp. 14):

40 *Skiff-building in the marshes, a scene from the tomb of Ti.*

The reed-floats of the sky are set in place for me
That I may cross on them to the horizon, to Ra. (FPT, Utt. 266)

A passage from Pliny the Elder writing in the first century AD informs us that such craft (*vitiles*) still remained a popular means of transport among the poorer classes in his day. These primitive craft were constructed from several bundles of papyrus reeds lashed together. There was usually a small, wooden platform amidships which supported the owner. Although such skiffs normally supported only one or two persons, tomb paintings show that larger craft existed which could transport cattle. They drew so little water that they were easily manoeuvrable even in shallow water. They were usually propelled along by hand or punted by pole. There is no evidence that they had sails, but the later appearance of the bipod mast, which was originally designed for use on much lighter craft, may indicate that such craft, occasionally, carried small sails. Such a belief may be supported by the existence of a hieroglyph depicting just such a mast on a papyrus skiff on a block from the so-called 'Room of Seasons' in the sun-temple of Nyuserra at Abu Ghurob.

Although the evidence would suggest that the Egyptians never ventured very far beyond the confines of their narrow valley, the scientist and adventurer, Dr Thor Heyerdahl, proved in 1970 that a 12m long modern replica of a papyrus craft built in the traditional way was durable enough to cross the Atlantic.

MIDDLE KINGDOM

Models and pictures of river boats from the Middle Kingdom show a considerable advance in ship design since the Sixth Dynasty. Boats were no longer flat bottomed with square angular ends but had round-bottomed, spoon-shaped hulls. The bow was practically horizontal but the stern rose quite steeply, often ending in a curved stern-piece designed specifically to support the loom of the steering-oar. The girdle-truss had disappeared and the deck-plan painted on models of the period show that longitudinal strength was provided by a central shelf or stringer which ran down the middle of the vessel at deck level. Lateral strength was provided by several transverse cross-beams which were jointed into the central stringer and which supported the removable deck-hatches (pl. VI). Model boats of the period often show a projecting, notched bow-strip which, it has been suggested, may have functioned as a fairlead for a mooring-rope.

By the Middle Kingdom, the bipod mast had disappeared and had been replaced by the pole mast which was stepped through the deck on the hull below. It was supported at deck level by a single, double, or even treble, knee-piece (fig. 41) and could be unstepped when not in use and stowed away on crutches. The mast had also moved closer to the mid-line of the boat which seems to imply that some attempt was now being made to use a wind on the quarter.

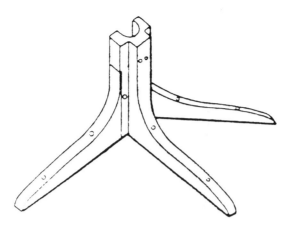

41 *Wooden model of mast support or 'knee'.*

The sail had also changed shape. It was broader than in the Old Kingdom and bent to a yard and boom. Since the latter no longer rested on the deck, its weight was supported in a series of lifts. These passed through a series of semicircular rings on either side of the mast near its top. These rings were frequently made of metal, but sometimes of wood or rope. The lifts for the boom passed through the lower set of rings and were secured either to a kind of rack on the deck just abaft the mast, or to a wooden attachment on the side of the steering-oar post. The boom was lashed to the mast, but the upper yard was free and could be lowered when taking-in sail. The forked spars used for extending the leeches of the sail had disappeared.

The sail-stitching was no longer horizontal as in the Old Kingdom, but vertical and more numerous. The yards were straight and were controlled by braces and sheets which were attached to rope-loops in the deck.

There was a fore-stay, but no back-stay, since the lifts for the yard which led back aft served that purpose. The mast was supported athwartships by a pair of shrouds.

42 *Steering oar with vertical tiller and horizontal cross-bar on a Middle Kingdom vessel.*

43 *Artist's impression of a Middle Kingdom boat voyaging on the Nile.*

The steering gear had also undergone a radical change and now consisted either of a single large oar mounted axially over the stern or, on larger vessels, of two steering-oars mounted on each quarter. The loom of the single type was lashed at mid-point either to the incurving stern-piece or to a block at the stern, while its butt-end was secured to the top of the steering-oar post on which it pivoted. Its degree of rotation was controlled by a tiller which reached down vertically abaft the rudder post (fig. 42). The looms of the double type were lashed above to the sides of vertical posts inset into a cross-beam on each quarter, while their looms, just above the shoulders of their blades, rested in grooves cut in the ends of a cross-beam which projected beyond the sides of the boat. As with the single type, their degree of rotation was controlled by sloping tillers dowelled into their looms.

On smaller boats, there were frequently small, round-topped shelters for the owner immediately forward of the steering-oar posts, although, on larger boats, quite elaborate deckhouses were built or arrangements were made for an awning.

The oarsmen were often provided with individual seats either in the shape of plain blocks or chairs with low backs. The oars were worked either in grommets or against thole-pins with inverted hooks.

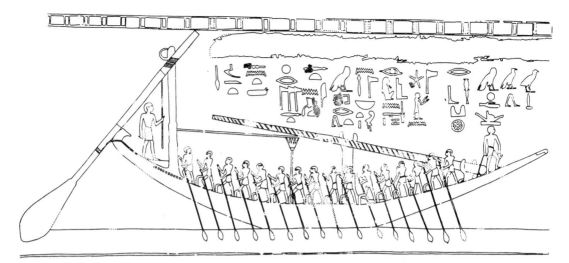

A good example of the new type of boat is to be found in the tomb of Senet, mother of Intefiqer who was vizier under Senusret I (fig. 44). The hull has a classic Middle Kingdom form: it is spoon shaped, round bottomed, and has a pointed prow and incurving stern. The vessel is steered by means of a single, centrally-mounted oar which is bound at mid-point to the stern which curves over inboard to support it. Its upper end is lashed to a ring or hook on the side of the tall steering-oar post. A rope wound around its loom safeguards it against loss. The helmsman stands on a small raised platform abaft the post and controls the oar with a long tiller. The mast has been unstepped and laid on two crutches, one amidships, probably in the vacated mast-hole, and another nearer the prow. An awning slung over posts with lotus-shaped finials occupies the aft portion of the deck. The boat is propelled by sixteen rowers whose oars are worked through grommets on thole-pins.

Papyriform boats

A good example of the Middle Kingdom 'pilgrimage boat' (front cover, pl. VII) is provided by a model from the British Museum. The boat displays the characteristic form which it was to retain henceforward, with minor changes, down to the end of the dynastic period. It is round bottomed and broad in the beam. The nearly vertical prow terminates at the top in a stylised papyrus umbel while the stern curves over inboard in a sickle-shape finial.

The mummy of the deceased lies on a bier amidships under a canopy with a curved roof. The vessel is steered by means of double steering-oars suspended over each quarter. These are supported on posts with falcon-head finials. A helmsman squats on the deck immediately abaft the steering-oar posts. Two female mourners stand at the head and foot of the mummy while, beside the bier, a lector-priest holding a rolled-up papyrus scroll in his hands, recites the appropriate magical spells which will ensure the deceased survival in the next life.

44 *Middle Kingdom sailing boat, from the tomb of Intefiqer.*

I *The ferryman of the dead, from the Book of the Dead of Ani.*

II *Mummy carried on a boat-shaped bier: vignette from the Book of the Dead of Ani.*

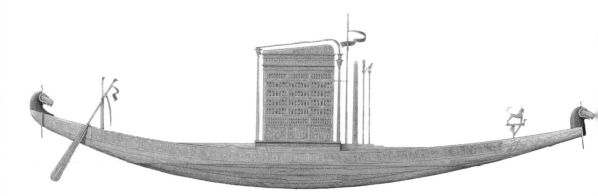

III *The Userhet, the ceremonial barge of the god Amun.*

IV *Sahure's ship.*

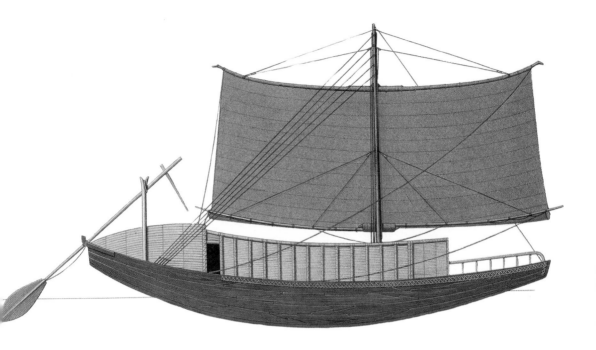

V *Old Kingdom cargo-boat.*

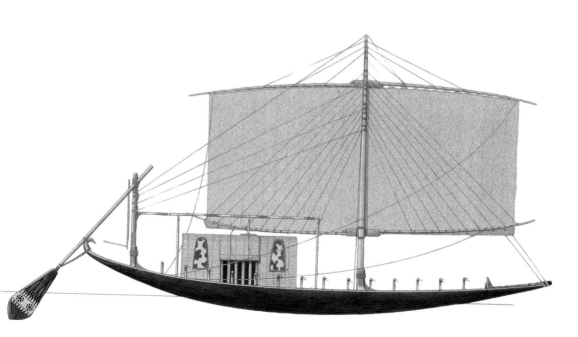

VI *Middle Kingdom sailing-boat depicted in the tomb of Intefiqer.*

VII *Model of a funerary bark with a mummy.*

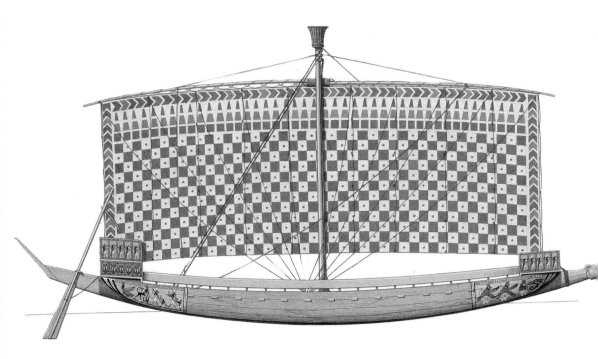

VIII *One of the Ramses III warships from his temple at Medinet Habu.*

New Kingdom

Although larger and more varied, New Kingdom boats were constructed in essentially the same way as their Middle Kingdom predecessors. The hulls were round bottomed and of shallow draught with a graceful sheer-line. They display a considerable overhang at stem and stern and are usually fitted with elongated finials with often curious notches beneath. It is difficult to determine their internal structure since paintings provide few details and the decks of the models of the period no longer display the characteristic red and white deck-plan (central-stringer, cross-beams and mast-hole) shown on their Middle Kingdom predecessors.

The deck was a foot or so below the edge of the gunwale except at each end. At the forward end it was flush and there was a break in the deck aft with a platform at the stern for the helmsmen. Deck-beams are commonly shown protruding through the planking along the sides of boats providing extra lateral support to the hull.

A single pole mast was stepped amidships through the deckhouse roof and, except in the smallest vessels, remained fixed. On smaller boats it could be unstepped whenever the boats were in port or under oar and stowed away with the yards and sail on the deckhouse roof. More often than not, the mast was left up and the upper yard and lower yard are shown together supported in lifts. It is uncertain how the mast was supported, since its base is usually concealed by the deckhouse. More than likely, as on earlier boats, its shaft was lashed securely to a stout cross-beam and further supported by a mast-step at deck level, while its heel was socketed into a transverse frame or a block on the hull bottom.

Masts of the New Kingdom had a rectangular frame or grid at the mast-head consisting of several horizontal and vertical cross-pieces through which the halyards ran, while immediately below there was a metal (?) sheath or comb with flanges on either side pierced with eye-holes to take the lifts which supported the yards. Although representations of boats under sail in the New Kingdom display a large number of ropes, it is often difficult to distinguish one from another because of the inaccuracies of the paintings and because vessels are often shown overlapping one another. Fore- and back-stays for supporting the mast are very much in evidence, but the absence of shrouds suggests that, probably, by this time, a more efficient method had been found of stabilising the mast on the hull bottom.

The lifts or ropes which support the upper yard are rarely shown, but these must have led from the upper eye-holes on the comb to the extremities of the yard on either side. In some scenes, these are often depicted hanging loose when the yard was raised. The lower lifts which supported the boom are nearly always shown and are generally very numerous. As in the late Old Kingdom and Middle Kingdom, they had the important role of supporting the weight of the boom which no longer rested on the deck and was now very long and heavy because of the considerable increase in the size of the sail. The lifts which supported the boom ran to the lower eye-holes on the comb.

Because of its increased size, the sail was bent to yards often made from two spars, scarfed and fished together at mid-point, which were nearly as long as the vessel itself. The upper yard was lowered when sail had to be taken in and a double halyard ran through the calcet and down to a rack on the deck immediately abaft the mast. The boom was always fixed high up on the mast above the deckhouse roof. It was secured to the mast by a parrel-lashing which allowed it to turn unhindered; but, although free to turn, it was not removable.

The rigging on one of the models discovered in Tutankhamun's tomb (no. 336) was so well preserved that it provides us with one of our best sources of evidence in the round for the period (fig. 45). As was the custom in the New Kingdom, the mast on the model is stepped through the deckhouse roof in the middle of the boat. The length of the mast from head to deck is about two-thirds of the length of the vessel. It is fitted with a upper halyard-block squared, with two eye-holes a side, and a lower comb, rounded, with four eye-holes a side. There are no shrouds or back-stays. The fore-stay (**B**) is knotted and looped around the mast-head above the upper block, then led downwards over the forward kiosk and made secure to the bows. As in the Hatshepsut boats, the boom is supported by eight topping-lifts (**K–K**) rigged as follows: no. 1 lift is made fast to the yard-arm with several turns and a half-hitch and passes through the uppermost hole in the starboard lower comb from aft to forward and is then made fast to the yard again forming no. 5 lift. Similarly, nos. 2 and 6, nos. 3 and 7 and nos. 4 and 8. The same method is used for the topping-lifts of the port-side yard arm. The sheets (**L–L**) are continuations of the lifts and lead aft, on the starboard side, from the 5th lift and, on the port-side, from the 4th lift. The yard is lashed to the mast by means of a parrel (**M**) which allows it to turn freely. The sail is attached to the upper yard arm with a continuous spiral lacing (**G–G**), while its foot must have been attached, when unfurled, to the boom. The halyards (**D–D**) consist of two ropes which are made fast to the upper yard a little to each side of its mid-point and then pass through the two lower holes in the halyard-block. From the mast-head they lead downwards and are made fast to the cross-piece which connects the steering-oar posts. The topping-lifts of the upper yard-arms (**E–E**) pass from forward aft through the upper holes of the halyard-block and are similarly secured to the cross-piece between the steering-oar posts. As was usual, both the boom and upper yard are made from two pieces, scarfed and fished together at mid-point, (**C–C, J–J**). Both yards are lashed together (**H**[1]). Braces (**F–F**) lead aft from each upper yard-arm. The sail is secured when furled by gaskets (**H**). The sail is made of linen dyed with madder, and is sewn vertically.

Many boats were elaborately decorated (see pp. 66–8). By Tutankhamun's time stalls were built on deck to house chariot horses. Often a second storey was added to the deckhouse roof with a staircase leading up

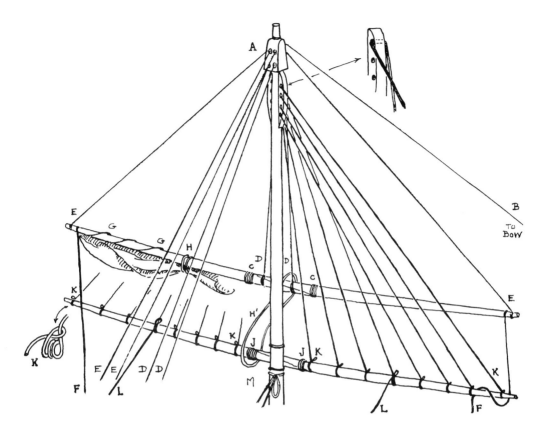

45 *Drawing of mast and rigging on a model sailing boat from the tomb of Tutankhamun.*

to it aft and porticos at each end supported on slender columns. Similarly the fore and after look-outs were extended and provided with canopies.

The oarsmen sat on the cross-thwarts on either side of the boat and worked their oars in grommets attached to thole-pins in the gunwale.

Deckhouses are found on nearly all the boats of the period. They are situated either amidships, built around the mast, or at the stern of the boat. These were rectangular in shape with curved roofs and, when unprovided with doors, were open at their narrower ends. Most often they were constructed of a frame covered with mats or of boarded-in walls probably finished with a rendering of plaster or gesso before painting. On large boats they were often two-tiered and could extend almost from stem to stern. The living quarters normally consisted of two or more compartments lit by several windows (fig. 46).

On the prow and stern were trapezoidal-shaped look-out platforms for the navigating officers (see pp. 70–71) which projected beyond the sides of the vessel and were enclosed with a rail on either side.

The steering-gear of the New Kingdom was generally of the same type as the Middle Kingdom. On smaller vessels, the butt-end of the oar rested in a fork at the top of a vertical post which was inset into a stout cross-beam in the after-deck, while its loom was mounted in a central forked-recess at the extreme stern of the vessel. Sometimes the point of

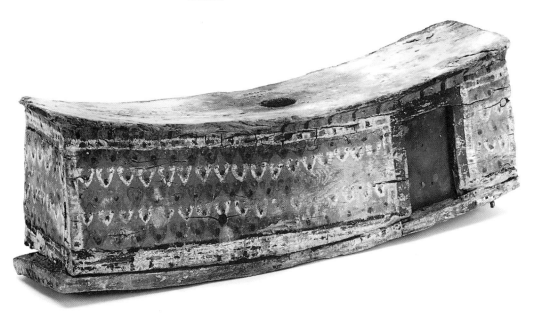

contact between post and oar is concealed by an animal skin, perhaps to keep the binding dry (fig. 47).

On the larger ships, and conventionally on funerary boats, the steering-gear consisted of two large oars suspended over either quarter and supported on vertical stanchions to which they were secured not only by plain lashings, but also by tackles of rope under tension secured to the ends of a stout cross-beam which protruded beyond the sides of the vessel.

46 *Decorated deckhouse from a New Kingdom model of a sailing boat.*

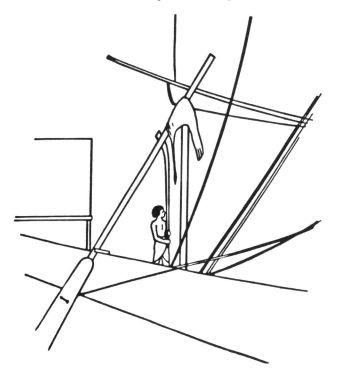

47 *Leather sleeve/guard covering the top of the steering-oar stanchion on a New Kingdom river vessel.*

The oars were also supported just above the shoulders of their blades by collars of stout rope or possibly leather fixed to the gunwales (see below, Hatshepsut). Their degree of rotation was controlled by tillers which descended downwards, sometimes forward, sometimes abaft the post.

It is not known for sure whether ballast was carried, but in view of the enormous spread of sail over a comparatively shallow hull, it would be reasonable to assume that ships were so weighted (see p. 68).

Sea-going ships

The reliefs of Queen Hatshepsut at Deir el-Bahri provide us with the clearest evidence for sea-going ships of the period. Although built in much the same way as river vessels, the hull of Hatshepsut's ship was decidely deeper than that of the Sahura ship and its lines were much more streamlined to meet the changed conditions (fig. 48, frontispiece). The girdle-truss had disappeared and extra athwartship support was provided by the deck-beams which protruded through the hull on either side just below the gunwale strake.

Breaks in the deck fore and aft provided slightly raised decks which were railed-in to give the crew protection in rough weather. There were look-outs on the fore- and after-decks protected by screens and decking over the centre-line of the vessel.

Instead of the more usual, elongated finials of river vessels, the bow ended in a solid, blade-shaped stem-piece while the stern curved over gracefully inboard ending in a lotus flower ornament. Perhaps this was intended to offset the danger of a following sea which could break over the ship's stern and swing her broadside on. However, because of the lack of a true keel, longitudinal strength had still to be provided by a hogging-

48 *Sailing boat of Hatshepsut from her mortuary temple at Thebes.*

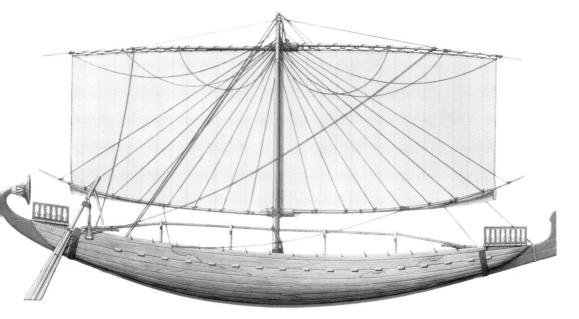

truss (see below). As with the riverine type, the ship was propelled by a low, broad sail suspended from a pole mast stepped amidships. The sail was bent to two yards which were made from two pieces of wood lashed together at mid-point. The lower yard was fixed to the mast with a parrel-lashing which allowed it to rotate freely about its axis.

There was a rectangular, grid-like structure at the mast-head which supported the double halyards. When the sail was hoisted, the halyards also helped to support the mast and doubled as preventer back-stays. The halyards were attached directly to the boom, on either side of its mid-point and made fast to the quarters. Braces controlled the angle of the upper yard and although, surprisingly enough, no sheets are shown in the reliefs, these must surely have existed to control the angle of the boom.

The lower yard was supported in sixteen lifts, eight a side, which led down from the comb on the lower half of the mast-head. Similarly, the upper yard was supported by an equal number of lifts, although, when hoisted, only two appear to have borne its full weight (fig. 49). Fore-and-aft support for the mast was provided by two fore-stays which were attached to the mast-head and made fast to either side of the bows, and a single back-stay which was attached to a cross-piece between the steering-oar posts. There were no shrouds, probably because the mast no longer needed such support.

There was no deckhouse which might upset the vessel's trim in rough weather and the sides of the fore- and aft-platforms followed the gunwale-line instead of projecting beyond it.

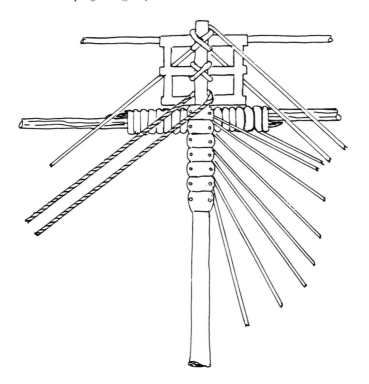

49 *Masthead rigging on Queen Hatshepsut's boat.*

50 *Drawing showing the arrangement of the double steering-gear on a New Kingdom sailing boat.*

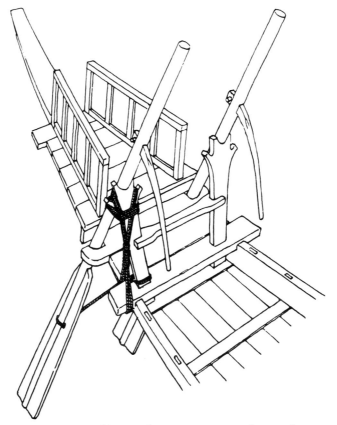

The ship was steered by two large oars mounted on each quarter (fig. 50). Their looms were mounted in forked stanchions and were lashed to the posts not only by plain bindings, but also by tackles of rope under tension secured to the ends of a protruding cross-beam. The oars were also held firmly in place just above the shoulders of their blades by collars of stout rope or leather, fixed to the gunwales. They were manipulated by long, curved, vertical tillers dowelled into their looms. The oarsmen sat behind the gunwales on either side and worked their oars through rope or leather grommets attached to the sides of the gunwales.

Longitudinal support for the hull was still provided for by the time-honoured system of the hogging-truss. Unlike the Sahura example, however, it was now a true cable and the means of obtaining tension had also been much improved. Although some details are still obscure, one scholar has proposed the following arrangement.

The cable was securely anchored at one end to a girt-rope that girdled the ship at the bow. It was then led back over two forked crutches to the mast, which served in place of the midships crutch on the Sahura boats, where it was secured by two tackles of twisted rope which encircled both the mast and the cable at their upper ends. Their lower ends were probably made fast to a cross-beam (**a, a**). By twisting the batons (**b, b**) the increased tension in the tackles would drag the hogging-truss down the mast, thereby providing the required degree of tautness. It was then led back aft from the mast along two crutches on the after-deck and secured to another girt-rope at the stern (fig. 51).

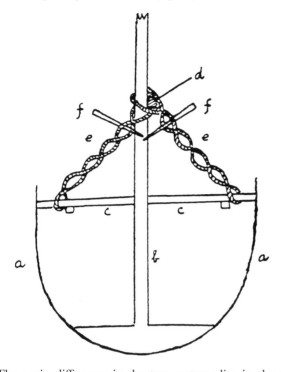

51 *Method of tightening a hogging-truss on a sea-going ship.*

a *Section of hull* **b** *Mast* **c** *Thwart* **d** *Section of hogging-truss* **e** *Rope tackles* **f** *Tensioning levers*

The main difference in the two systems lies in the method used to regulate the tension. In the Old Kingdom this was obtained with the help of one or more wooden batons inserted into the strands of the truss and twisted – thereby shortening its length – until the desired degree of tautness was obtained. However, by the New Kingdom, or earlier, the Ancient Egyptians had improved on this system by attaching two tackles of twisted rope on either side of the mast above the truss. Wooden batons were used, as in the Old Kingdom, to shorten the tackles thereby indirectly affecting the tautness of the hogging-truss. There were two advantages to this method. First, the tensioning could be better regulated since one revolution of the truss corresponded to several turns of the rope-tackles and, secondly, the tackles also provided athwartship support to the mast.

More recently, the German scholar, Biess, has proposed a different method of fastening for the truss on the Hatshepsut boats. He believes that, instead of being secured to girt-ropes fore and aft, the ends of the hogging-truss were made fast to transverse deck-beams in the prow and stern. The girt-ropes would not, therefore, have functioned simply as points of attachment for the truss, but would have had the important task of compressing the hull-planking at its most vulnerable points to prevent the deck-beams from being pulled out under the enormous pressure.

Cargo boats

The hulls of New Kingdom cargo boats were similar to those of passenger boats, except that they were often more beamy and did not display any finials at bow and stern. They had a central steering-oar mounted in a longitudinal forked recess at the extreme stern. Some scenes show a curious oblong-shaped fixture attached to the butt-end of the steering-oar. This, it has been suggested, may have acted as a counterweight to facilitate the elevation of the oar out of the water. There was a cargo-house amidships usually walled by lattice but open to the sky and, aft of this, a small, semicircular shelter for the crew.

The masts and rigging were similar to other New Kingdom vessels, and when not in use were taken down and laid on top of the deckhouse roof. Quant poles were carried to help ease the boats off sandbanks. Their ends curled over like huge walking sticks which could be fitted against the shoulder to give better leverage (Huy, Neferhotep, Kenamun).

Papyriform boats

Papyriform (funerary) boats appear little altered from the Twelfth Dynasty. They were broad and of very shallow draught with ornamental decorative finials at bow and stern. Amidships was a level platform on which stood a canopy supported on four light columns. Beneath this the statues of the deceased and his wife are usually shown undertaking a journey to one of the sacred sites. There were small steering-oars with decorated blades on the quarters supported on posts (fig. 52).

52 *Pilgrimage scene from the tomb of Amenemhet at Thebes.*

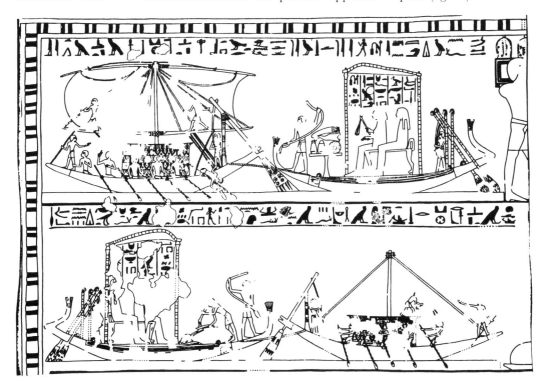

This type of boat was never rowed or sailed but was always towed either by another vessel or by a company of men from the bank.

LATE NEW KINGDOM

Although the evidence becomes increasingly more sparse after the New Kingdom, the vessels shown in the celebrations of the Ipet festival in the reigns of Ramses III (1194–1163 BC) and Herihor of the Twentieth Dynasty (1080–1070 BC) display the same features as earlier boats (figs 53, 54). As in the earlier period, the hulls retained their traditional shape and the steering-oars were mounted in clefts at the stern and lashed to vertical forked stanchions. The masts amidships were supported by stout forked mast-steps (Herihor) and, although they were not provided with deckhouses, there were elaborate kiosks on their fore-decks. The ends of the cross-beams still protruded through the sides of planking (Ramses not Herihor) on either side and their broad sails were bent to yards made of two separate spars lashed together at mid-point. Unfortunately, the rigging is so cursorily drawn (Ramses III) that it is well-nigh impossible to determine what ropes there were, but their mast-heads still show the same arrangement as on earlier ships: a mast-block for the halyards and beneath a calcet for supporting the lifts to the lower and upper yards. No fore- and after-stays are shown, but their omission may well owe more to the negligence of the artists than to historical fact.

53 *Boats towing the royal 'galley' of Ramses.*

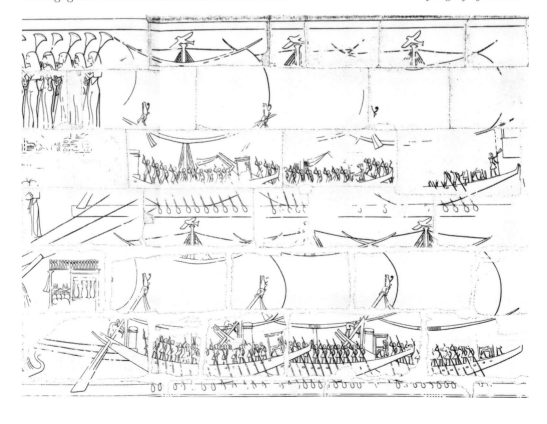

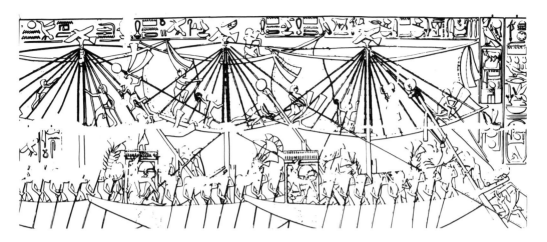

54 *Boats towing the great barge Mery-Amun on the Nile during the Opet Festival of Herihor.*

Warships

Perhaps some of the most famous vessels dating to the late New Kingdom are the warships which Ramses III (1194–1163 BC) employed against the Sea Peoples. These are depicted on one of the outer walls of his mortuary temple at Medinet Habu (fig. 55, pl. VIII). Even when due allowance has been made for developments in traditional ship design, there can be little doubt that they exhibit several new features which were to appear later in a more developed form in the ships of Phoenicia, Greece and Rome. The hulls are long and low and are provided with raised bulwarks or screens, with holes for the oars, rigged along each gunwale to protect the rowers from enemy missiles. The prows end in lion figure-heads, while the sterns are more elevated than in earlier vessels to give a better all-round view to the helmsman. Although it has been claimed that these lion figure-heads are the first example of the use of a ram in naval warfare, this is unlikely in view of the technique used to construct Egyptian boats. Since there is no evidence that the hulls of these 'fighting-ships' were constructed in any way differently from earlier vessels – the presence of protruding cross-beams point to this – then these boats would have been built 'shell-first' with the result that they would not have had sufficient structural strength to absorb the shock of ramming other vessels and would have buckled and collapsed on impact.

A raised gangway which provided an unobstructed fighting area for the marines seems to have run the whole length of the ship and the deck was carried on cross-beams which protruded through the hull in the traditional way.

No hogging-trusses are visible on any of the ships which may perhaps suggest that either their internal structural design had been much improved, or that better materials had been used in their construction. As in earlier times, the mast was stepped amidships, but it now had a fighting top from which the occupant could keep watch or hurl down projectiles on to an enemy.

The square sail was narrower than in earlier times, but was still bent to

55 *New Kingdom warship. A detail of the sea battle of Ramses III against the Sea Peoples from the mortuary temple at Medinet Habu.*

a upper yard. The boom had been dispensed with and, contrary to previous practice, the sail was furled by hoisting its foot to the upper yard, where it was secured just below the fighting top, presumably to keep it out of the way of the fighting men during an engagement and to prevent its use as a means of boarding when manoeuvring under oar. The loose-footed sail with its vertical brailing ropes was a decided advance over the older form of rig and was probably introduced in the late New Kingdom. It had many advantages over the older form in that it furnished immediate and complete control of the sail from the deck, and also permitted the shortening of selected areas of the sail which increased the ship's manoeuvrability.

Our evidence would suggest that the Egyptians had begun to use this type of sail as early as the beginning of the Twentieth Dynasty. Two vignettes on fragments of papyrus in the Turin Museum, dated loosely to the late New Kingdom, show Nile boats fitted with what may be a transitional stage of the rig. The sails of these boats have brails like the Medinet Habu ships, but with the difference that, as with the traditional rig, they are not loose-footed, but have two yards which curve upwards at their extremities. What may be another example of brailing ropes appear on a fragment of a relief from Saqqara dating to the late Eighteenth Dynasty now in the Berlin Museum. The use of loose-footed sails similar to those on Ramses III's ships is attested much later in reliefs in the temple of Edfu in Ptolemaic times (Main Pylon, east side) and Herodotus refers to the rings and brailing ropes used to reef this type of sail in his day (*Histories* II, 36, 4 and here, fig. 56).

The ropes of the rigging had also undergone considerable change. They were much simpler, and the yard was no longer suspended in numerous lifts. The braces were attached to the extremities of the upper yard and led back aft to the helmsman's platform.

The warships were steered by a helmsman who sat on a raised platform at the stern. A similar platform in the bows provided a vantage point for

56 *The god Horus on a boat equipped with a loose-footed sail, from the temple of Edfu.*

the archers. The ships were steered by two large oars suspended over each quarter with their tillers horizontal above the platform for easy handling.

There is no evidence that the innovations shown in the Medinet Habu relief (the new style of hull, the mast with simplified staying, a fighting top and the loose-footed sail) were borrowed by the Egyptians from neighbouring countries. Although their straight profile and angular ends seem at first sight to have their origin in the Aegean world – the duck-head figure-head appears on a Greek vase of slightly later date – there is no compelling reason to ascribe such developments to an external influence and just as good a case can be made for native Egyptian ingenuity.

Apart from the Piy (formerly read Piankhi) relief (see below), after the Ramesside period we have very little information about boats until Graeco-Roman times. The boats depicted in the temple of Horus at Edfu accompanying the sacred barge of Hathor of Dendera during the reign of Ptolemy VIII (170–163, 145–116 BC) show little change in their general design from earlier Nile boats. Their prows and sterns are cut off square and their deck beams protrude through the planking on to the outside of the hull. There are look-out platforms on the prow and stern and the steering-oars with their long tillers are mounted in clefts at their sterns. A tall mast is stepped amidships supported by stays. A similar scene on the opposite wall showing the departure of the same flotilla south under sail clearly depicts the same type of loose-footed sail used earlier on the warships of Ramses III.

KING'S SHIP-OF-STATE

Apart from some early drawings of boats on vases of the Early Dynastic Period from Abydos, perhaps the earliest reference, albeit inferred, to a royal ship-of-state occurs in the title 'Director of the king's ship' which appears on the stela of the official Merka dating to the reign of Qa'a of the First Dynasty.

Although the Palermo Stone records that a royal ship called the *Adoration-of-the-Two-Lands* of 100 cubits in length (52.5m) was constructed in the reign of Sneferu, and a similarly named vessel is mentioned much earlier on a vase from the pyramid of Djoser (2630–2611 BC) of the Third Dynasty, it is not until we come to the Fifth Dynasty that we are given our first glimpse of a real ship-of-state. Only the immensely tall sail covered with an intricate star-like pattern and the forward portion of the ship survives today, but it is sufficient to show how grand such vessels were as they sailed along the Nile (fig. 57).

The hull has a gently curving sheer and is surmounted by a washstrake amidships which stops just short of the prow. Like the Khufu boat, it has a tall, delicately carved, lotus-bud finial surmounted by a solar disk at the prow and, although the stern section is missing, we may safely assume that this was similarly provided with a sickle-shaped finial which curved over inboard. On the forward deck stands a royal sphinx on a standard, while immediately abaft is a baldachin containing the king's(?) throne. Although propelled by a tall sail, the heads of the oarsmen can be seen protruding above the gunwale. A protective *udjat*-eye is painted on the prow and most probably there was originally a deckhouse or an awning supported on columns amidships.

It is not until we reach the New Kingdom that we are again provided with representations of such large ships. Apart from the splendid river vessels belonging to such high officers of state as Rekhmira and Huy, the only ships of state which can be securely associated with the king himself are those represented by the models of Amenhotep II and Tutankhamun.

Royal ships of the New Kingdom, such as the *Beloved-of-Amun* (fig. 58) have gently curving sheers, elevated towards the stern, ending in elongated finials. Streamers are attached to the prow and stern. The crossbeams which protrude through the planking on either side, end in carved heads. There are elaborate kiosks on the prow and stern decorated with figures of the king trampling upon his enemies. A large double-roofed deckhouse is situated amidships with doors and windows along its sides. *Uraei* and a double ovoid-shaped frieze decorates the upper edges of the roof. Priests holding fans and feathered wands stand on deck while sixty rowers, thirty on either side, row the ship. A tall mast is stepped amidships through the deckhouse roof and the ship is steered by two large steering-oars with long, vertical tillers suspended over each quarter. The large, broad sail is bent to two long yards made of two separate spars and suspended in numerous lifts. On the mast-head stands a royal falcon-standard with outstretched wings.

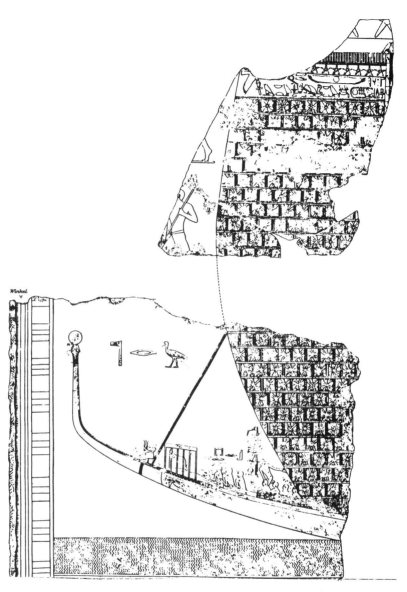

57 *King Sahura's ship-of-state.*

Although pictorial evidence is limited, several royal ships are referred to, or named, in our literary sources. During his struggle against the Hyksos leader Apophis, King Kamose of the Seventeenth Dynasty (*c.*1555–1550 BC) records on his stela that he 'caused the mighty *mek*-ship to sound the desert edge, the fleet after it as it were a kite'. Later, Amenhotep II (1427–1401 BC) records how he hanged seven enemy princes head-downwards from the prow of his falcon ship, *Akheprura-is-the-Establisher-of-the-Two-Lands* (BAR II, §797).

In more peaceful times, Amenhotep III commanded that a lake be dug 'for the Great King's Wife Tiy ... His majesty celebrated the feast of the opening of the lake ..., when his majesty sailed thereon in the royal barge

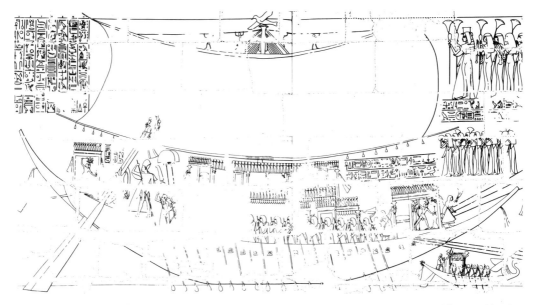

58   *The great ship-of-state, Mery Amun, in the Ipet Festival at Luxor, from a relief at Karnak.*

Aten-Gleams' (BAR II, §869). Several royal ships are also mentioned in association with the officers or infantrymen who served aboard them: *Akheperura-endures, Ramses II Who-Propitiates-the-Aten, Merenptah Beloved-of-Sekhmet, The Aten-Gleams, Star-of-Memphis* and so on. During his long and distinguished career, the standard-bearer of the king's ship, *Beloved-of-Amun,* Ahmose, son of Abana, who lived in the early part of the Eighteenth Dynasty, served on several ships before ending his career on the *Rising-in-Memphis.* A later version of the *Beloved-of-Amun* is pictured on an axe-head now in the British Museum. The inscription on its blade identifies its owner as the infantryman, Nehmem, who served aboard the vessel during the reign of Amenhotep II.

In the Twenty-Fifth Dynasty, King Piy (750–712 BC) had the return of his expedition from the south to Thebes recorded on a wall of the Temple of Mut at Karnak. Among them was a large vessel described in the accompanying text as 'the ship of Piy' which was 43 cubits (22.6m) in length.

OBELISK BARGES

No survey of Ancient Egyptian shipping would be complete without a brief mention of a special type of vessel used by the Ancient Egyptians from an early period to transport heavy loads. These were the giant barges used to convey obelisks and other building materials from the sites where they were quarried to the temples and tombs throughout the length and breadth of Egypt.

The earliest evidence for such barges comes from a block from Unas' (2356–2323 BC) causeway which shows parts of three large boats bringing granite columns from the quarries at Aswan to his pyramid complex at

Saqqara. The columns are securely lashed to their sledges ready for easy conveyance to their final location (fig. 59).

In his tomb biography Weni, who lived in the Sixth Dynasty, tells us that the Pharaoh Merenra (2255–2246 BC) sent him to bring a false door, lintels, and portals for his pyramid in six barges and three tow-boats of eight ribs. Some time later, the same king commissioned him to build a 'broad-boat' of 60 cubits (31.5m) in length and 30 cubits (15.75m) in breadth of local acacia to transport an offering-table from the alabaster quarry at Hatnub in Middle Egypt, (BAR I, §323). Similarly, Sened-jemib-inti, who was vizier under Djedkara Isesi of the Fifth Dynasty, (2388–2356 BC), used a cargo boat strengthened with a girdle-truss to transport his king's sarcophagus and lid from Tura to Giza.

During the reign of Tuthmose I (1504–1492 BC), Ineni supervised the construction of an 'august boat' of 120 cubits (63m) in length and 40 cubits (21m) in breadth to transport obelisks to the Temple of Karnak. These obelisks can still be seen today and together weigh 372 tons.

Perhaps the most famous example of such a barge is to be found in the funerary temple of Queen Hatshepsut (1473–1458 BC) at Deir el-Bahari, which shows the transportation of two giant obelisks from Aswan to Karnak (fig. 60). Several scholars have attempted to calculate the exact size of the barge by employing the known weight of the obelisks which have survived. Unfortunately, it has proved impossible to arrive at any firm conclusion, and figures ranging from 84m in length and 28m in breadth with a displacement under load of 2,664 tons (according to Koster, *Studien*, 1f) to a more modest 63m in length, and 25m in breadth with a displacement under load of 1,500 tons (according to Solver, *Obelisk-skibe*, 29ff) have been proposed. However, if recent research challenging the identification of the actual obelisks used in the calculations is correct, then the figures have to be revised upwards with the result that we are confronted with a barge with the almost unbelievable dimensions of 95m in length, with a beam of 32m and a displacement with cargo of 7,300 tons!

Whatever its size, however, such a vessel would have been built using the same traditional shell-first technique used for other more modest

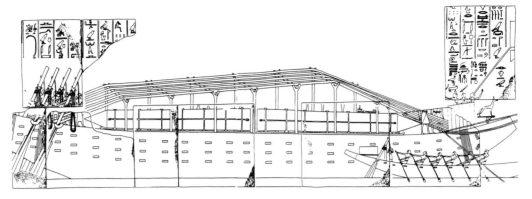

60 *Queen Hatshepsut's obelisk barge.*

vessels, although greatly scaled-up to provide a structure which could support the extra weight. The relief allows us to draw some tentative conclusions about its construction. Three tiers of cross-beams served to give lateral strength to the massive hull, while longitudinal strength was provided by five hogging-trusses supported on forked posts which spanned the length of the vessel and were made fast to girt-ropes which encircled the hull fore and aft. We may assume that the weight of the obelisks would have been supported by the cross-beams and central shelves extending the length of the vessel. In his book, *Ships of the Pharaohs*, Landström has suggested a total of six shelves: two in the mid-line and two underneath each obelisk. The hull bottom and sides were probably strengthened, as in the Khufu boat, by a series of 'passive' frames inset into the hull bottom at regular intervals.

Because of its enormous size, the barge was steered, unusually for the period, by two oars suspended over each quarter. It was towed by thirty boats propelled by eight hundred and sixty-four oarsmen deployed in three columns. The exact method used to tow the barge remains problematic and the various methods proposed to date remain unconvincing.

Uncertainty also surrounds the technique used by the Ancient Egyptians to load such heavy weights. According to a passage in Pliny, describing the transport of an obelisk to Alexandria in Ptolemaic times, a canal was first dug beneath an obelisk and then a barge, loaded with sufficient ballast to lower its height in the water, was floated beneath it. The ballast was then removed to allow it to take the full weight of the obelisk. More recently, a different solution has been proposed. According to this, the barge was brought as near to the bank of the river as possible and an embankment was constructed around and over it. The obelisk was then man-handled up the embankment until it was directly over the barge and let down into place by removing the fill around the barge (Habachi, *Obelisks*, p. 27 following an earlier author).

DECORATION

It is not until we reach the New Kingdom that ships begin to be elaborately decorated. Prior to this, decoration was usually limited to a few narrow sheer-lines running parallel with the gunwale on the hull or to polychrome transverse stripes on masts, cabin supports, steering-oar posts and oar-looms. The walls of the cabins were decorated with a simple chequerboard pattern and the blades of the steering-oars were adorned with blue and white lotus flowers and sacred *udjat*-eyes. Small boats and freight boats of the New Kingdom were either left plain or were painted a simple uniform colour. On larger river vessels, the mid-section of the hull was usually left plain, but the stems and sterns were often decorated with various designs which could range from a very stylised flower or plant design to a more complex mythological scene or a mixture of both. These often combine with other patterns: horizontal bands enclosing a chequer board or geometric pattern, circles or rosettes, horizontal bands and squares with small black points in their centres, and narrow, transverse bands of colour encircling the hull without any other decoration. An excellent example of such abstract hull decoration occurs on one of the Tutankhamun models (no. 276) while a more complex mythological decoration can be seen on another (no. 284).

A painting from the Tomb of Rekhmira shows a large sailing ship which is decorated with a mixed design of plant and mythological scenes. The panel on the underside of the prow contains an *udjat*-eye followed by falcons on pedestals. The stern is similarly decorated except that a kneeling figure of Maat with outstretched wings is added. The hull, fore and aft, is also decorated with narrow transverse bands containing an abstract plant design.

Ships decorated with purely mythological scenes are well illustrated by models from the Tomb of Amenhotep II (1427–1401 BC) and paintings from the tomb of Huy.

Deckhouses were not decorated with mythological figures even on ships of a decidedly religious character (Qenamun, Huy, Menna). Normally, the decoration consisted of patterns of various coloured circles, stylised fronds and chequerboard patterns enclosed at the top and sides with narrow, block-patterned dados. The side-panels of the look-out platforms were also decorated with different variations of the chequerboard design. On royal ships, however, these could be more elaborately decorated either with paintings of sphinxes, lions and bulls, or with representations of the same animals carved out of the wood.

Boats such as the royal ships-of-state, temple barges and those owned by great state officials, were more intricately decorated with religious scenes. The hull of Huy's great ship was adorned with *udjat*-eyes, the head of the ram of Amun, winged falcons on pedestals and the king as a sphinx trampling on his fallen enemies. The sides of the look-outs were decorated with striding figures of Mont, the Theban god of war, while the deckhouse walls were covered with an intricate pattern of multi-coloured circles framed at top and bottom with narrow block-patterned dados. The blades of the steering-oars were decorated with blue and white lotuses, roundels and *udjat*-eyes.

Sails were often decorated with diverse patterns. The sail of Sahura's ship was decorated with a pattern of adjoining squares arranged in brick-like fashion enclosing eight-pointed stars within circles. Later scenes show sails decorated with yellow circles within alternating red and white squares and plain red squares on a white background.

The mid-section of the hulls of funerary vessels were usually painted green with gold-coloured finials at prow and stern. Their bulwarks were decorated with blue and red sheer-lines. The looms of their steering-oars and the posts which supported them were often decorated with parallel, multi-coloured bands, while the blades of the oars were adorned with stylised lotus blossoms and narrow bands containing *udjat*-eyes.

PADDLING/ROWING

Egyptian vessels were paddled, rowed or poled. Paddling, in which the paddler first raised the blade above his head and then leaned over the side to reach the water, required great stamina. The stroke was not simultaneous, but each man dipped his blade in the water a fraction of a second behind the man in front in a sinuous, wave-like motion (fig. 61). Scenes from the temple of Hatshepsut at Deir el-Bahari, showing the different positions adopted by Ancient Egyptian oarsmen, serve as our main source of evidence for the technique used by them at this period. The oar was suspended in a loop or grommet of leather over the ship's side and

61 *Paddlers, from a relief in the funerary temple of King Userkaf.*

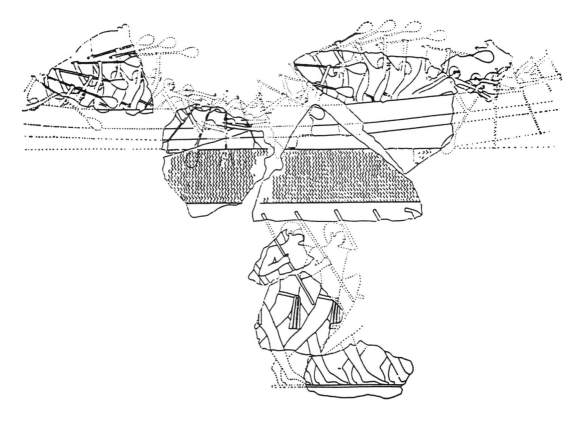

was held by the oarsman in a double-handed grip. The rowing technique consisted of a circular movement where the oarsman alternatively stood and sat as he rowed the boat along. The oarsman started his stroke in a standing position, then reached well forward and threw his weight back on the oars simultaneously taking up a sitting position on the cross-bench. Towards the end of the stroke, the hands were pushed downwards and the blade of the oar brought slowly out of the water before the stroke was recommenced. In order to provide the necessary leverage for this continuous circular movement, the oarsman's feet must either have been secured to the deck in loops or wedged under the stretchers in front of him. Because of the wear and tear that such a technique inflicted on his clothing, the rower wore a network garment with a square leather patch on the seat over his kilt to protect the fabric from the continuous chafing.

EQUIPMENT

Navigational aids, as one would expect on vessels primarily designed to operate in a river environment, were practically non-existent. As in later times, sea-going ships probably hugged the coastline for their bearings and protection. Reliefs show that each boat had a look-out on its prow who carried a long pole to sound the depth of water beneath the hull or to push the boat away from any obstruction which might endanger its safety. Paintings and models also show that landing-planks, mooring-stakes, mallets and fenders were carried. Trapezoidal slabs with holes at their narrower upper ends to take a cable or rope are frequently shown on the bows and sterns of Old Kingdom boats. But, although several such mooring-stones have been discovered in Egypt, their identification is still very much a matter of debate among scholars, and all attempts to identify the Egyptian word for an anchor have so far failed.

BALLAST

Although no information is available from Ancient Egypt, it must be assumed that, because of their shallow keels, rather flat bottoms and enormous spread of sail, Egyptian boats could not have sailed light or they would have been in danger of capsize. Larger vessels must, therefore, have been weighted with ballast of some kind to ensure that they maintained their trim. The Ancient Egyptians may have used stone to provide the required stability, as found in the bilges of classical wrecks, but the cargo itself could also have served as ballast. Care had also to be taken to ensure that the ballast was correctly distributed in the hold since its movement could precipitate the very disaster that its presence was designed to prevent. In Ancient Egyptian ships ballast probably occupied all the available space under the deck-planking. Consequently, although one cannot rule out the dictates of artistic convention, the cargo on Egyptian ships is usually shown stowed on deck and secured firmly with ropes.

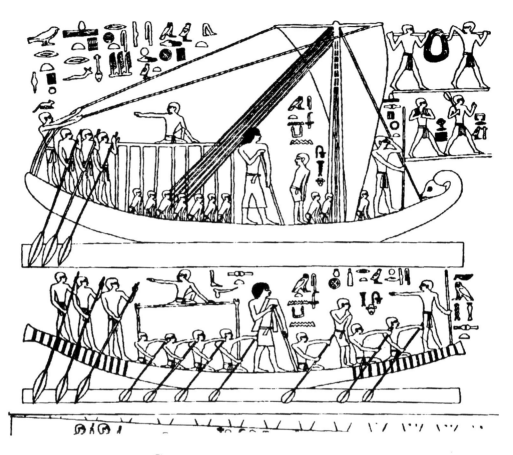

CREW MEMBERS

The evidence provided by pictures and models show that, beside a crew of ordinary sailors (*seqedu, nefeu*), each boat, depending on its class, had two officers who were responsible for its navigation. The first was the pilot or bow-officer (*ash-hat, sa en imyet-hat, imey-hat*), who stood watch in the forward lookout in the bows and was responsible for giving directions to the helmsman and for testing the depth of water beneath the hull with a sounding pole. The second was the helmsman (*hemu, irey-hemyt*), who stood or squatted in the stern of the boat between the steering-oars and was reponsible for steering the boat.

A third group of individuals who must also have held an important position on board were those who are often depicted standing or squatting on the deckhouse roof, holding a kind of baton or whip in one hand while gesturing with the other as if giving orders. These are probably to be identified with the 'Directors of a ship's contingent of rowers' (*kherep henyt*) who were responsible for regulating the oar-stroke and for relaying the pilot's commands to the helmsman. The remainder of the crew consisted of ordinary sailors, who either sat on the port and starboard sides facing the prow when paddling or, alternatively, sat and stood facing aft when rowing. When not engaged in any specific task, such as hoisting

62 *Two boats from the tomb of Ni-ka-nesut.*

sail and tightening stays, they would have busied themselves with the daily routine of running a ship.

Examples of such officers can be seen in an Old Kingdom scene from the tomb of Ni-ka-nesut at Giza which shows a lookout on the prow with a sounding-pole and a man on the cabin roof (*seshem*) giving directions or relaying orders to three helmsmen in the stern (fig. 62).

Little is known about the size of a ship's complement. Their number probably varied according to the size and type of boat. A crew of 120 men is mentioned in the *Tale of the Shipwrecked Sailor* (early Twelfth Dynasty), while more than 200 are mentioned on the Sphinx Stela of Amenhotep II. These were large boats and it is probable that most river vessels had a crew of around twenty-five men. The model sailing boats found in the tomb of Meketra had crews of sixteen men including their captains.

CHAPTER FOUR

Boat building

Woodworking techniques

Although objects made of wood have been discovered from the Predynastic Period, fine woodworking only became possible with the invention of copper tools in the Early Dynastic Period. All the principles of working in wood were known and used at an early date and, although the tools were few, they nevertheless fulfilled all the essential functions of modern carpentry. Among those which have survived from this period are chisels, saws, squares, levels and mallets which differ little from those in use today. Nothing comparable to the modern-day hammer has yet been found, but it is probable that they were of the wooden maul or club-like variety used in later times to drive in mooring-stakes. The jack plane was unknown in ancient Egypt until Roman times, but the adze was more than an adequate substitute in the hands of a skilled craftsman. The saw used by the Egyptians was of the pull variety, that is to say, the cutting edge of the teeth was set towards the handle and the cut was made on the pull, and not on the push. Small pieces of wood could be easily worked by being held upright by the hand, but heavier timber was lashed to a post and kept firmly in place by a tourniquet – a stick weighted with a heavy stone – leaving the carpenter free to use both hands. Bradawls and bow-drills were used for making holes. The drill was held upright, its top turning in half a dom-palm nut held in one hand, while the bit was rapidly rotated with a bow held in the other. Because of the softness of the copper tools, an oil flask and honing stone were also an indispensable part of the carpenter's equipment. Adzes and sandstone rubbers were used to obtain a smooth, even surface and measurements could be checked with a square, level or plumb line.

Wood of sufficient size and quality was always a scarce commodity in Egypt and profoundly affected carpentry techniques. It was carefully cut into lengths and joined by a variety of joints: dovetailing and cramps, mitre and mortise-and-tenon. Separate pieces were also dowelled or lashed together with leather thongs. Boat building was no exception to this, and for large vessels, such as the Khufu boat, shipbuilders had to go elsewhere to procure timber of sufficient length and quality, and records show that from an early date supplies had to be imported, notably from the Lebanon.

Sneferu (2575–2551 BC) of the Fourth Dynasty records the arrival of a convoy of forty ships laden with *meru*-wood from the Lebanon. So strong was the connection between the country of origin of timber and the process of boat building dependent upon it, that the Egyptians named their sea-going ships 'Byblos-ships', a term which was still in use in the Late Period to describe Nekau's newly introduced Greek triremes. Even in the *Coffin Texts* the deceased is said to punt with a pole made from the 'cedar' of Byblos (FCT I, Sp. 62) and during his Asiatic campaigns, Tuthmose III (1479–1425 BC) built cargo vessels of the same wood, obtained from the same locality.

BOAT BUILDING

Apart from the mention of a dockyard on an ivory tablet of the late Second Dynasty, the earliest representation of the construction of a wooden boat in a workshop comes from the early Fourth Dynasty mastaba of Rahotep at Meidum where a group of workmen is shown busy at work on a papyriform wooden boat (fig. 63). Perhaps the most famous scene is to be found in the Fifth Dynasty tomb of the vizier Ti. The now partly destroyed caption describes the scene as the '[. . . construction of] *shabet*-boats by the carpenters of the funerary estate' (fig. 64). One boat has rounded ends, another has a sharp-pointed stern while yet another is cut-off square at each end. Their hulls are supported on short batons during construction. The accompanying inscriptions list the several types of carpentry tools being used: adze, chisel, pull-saw, axe and club-shaped maul. The workers also use large oblong pounders(?), perhaps to hammer the strakes down into place. The carpenters are engaged in the different tasks of boat building. In the bottom register, on the left, one group is hewing a piece of rough timber into shape while, in the centre, another is

63 *Boat-building scene from the tomb of Rahotep at Meidum.*

attaching a bulwark to the topmost strake. On the right, one carpenter is busy sawing a piece of timber, while two others, seated astride a finished plank, appear to be preparing mortises in its upper surface with chisels and mauls. The 'Elder of the Workshop' (*semsu wekhret*) occupies a prominent position in the middle of the scene. He holds a ferrule and lead with which to check the accuracy of the hull curves.

A similar scene occurs in the tomb of Mereruka of the Sixth Dynasty, which shows two wooden papyriform boats under construction. The workmen use tools similar to those in Ti's tomb. A carpenter checks the boat's dimensions with a plumb-bob while two others stretch a measuring-line(?) from stem to stern. The caption informs us that the two papyriform vessels are *shabet*-boats constructed of *ished*-wood with which the deceased will journey to the 'Beautiful West'.

Not much evidence of the initial stages of boat building has survived, but it can be safely assumed that, as with other crafts, boat building was a traditional occupation whose skills were passed down verbally from father to son.

Because only short lengths of wood could be obtained locally, Egyptian carpenters were forced to devise a method of fitting or tenoning the hulls together which did not use long lengths of timber. Just such a method of construction is depicted in the tomb of Khnumhotep (Twelfth Dynasty)

64 *Boat-building scene from the tomb of Ti at Saqqara.*

65 *Boat-building scene from the tomb of Khnumhotep at Beni Hasan.*

at Beni Hasan (fig. 65), while, around a thousand years later, Herodotus describes essentially the same method of boat building in his day:

> ***Their freighters are constructed of acacia ... From this acacia, then, they cut planks about two cubits long [1.05m] and fit them together after the fashion of brickwork, building their ships in the following way: they fix the two-cubit planks around long tenons set close together. When they have built their ship in this way, they stretch thwarts over them [sc. the planks]. They do not use ribs. They caulk the seams from within with papyrus. (Herodotus, Histories II, §96; Lloyd, Classical Quarterly, vol. 29, no. 1 (May 1979), p.48)***

From this it is evident that, in contrast to the modern-day method of boat building, the Ancient Egyptian did not use a pre-erected framework of a keel and ribs on to which to fasten the planking ('skeleton/frame-first' build), but laid down a shell of planks in brick-like fashion into which they later inserted cross-beams at regular intervals to provide lateral strengthening to the hull (that is, 'shell-first' build). It is not known when this technique was first introduced, but Egypt is a strong contender as its place of origin. The modern technique of fastening the planking to a pre-erected framework of a keel and ribs was not introduced until the Middle Ages.

Information as to how the Ancient Egyptians set about building their boats is provided by actual hulls which have survived. The shipwright began his hull with a sort of keel-plank made of several lengths which formed the centre-line of the whole construction. Short planks were added on either side, fastened edge-to-edge by means of mortises-and-tenons or dovetail cramps, or a combination of both. When the shell of planks had reached the required height, the whole construction was finished off with gunwales and a series of cross-beams inlet into the uppermost strake on either side. These beams not only supported the weight of the deck-planking, but also served to provide athwartship support to the hull and prevent the sides from sagging outwards. On larger boats the hull was often strengthened by the addition of a central shelf or stringer which extended the whole length of the boat from stem to stern just under the cross-beams. This was supported by vertical stanchions inset into the frames at the bottom of the hull. Sometimes the shell was braced by the insertion of several 'passive' strengthening frames. The planks were set carvel fashion, that is, edge-to-edge, and never overlapped, as in clinker-built ships.

Although some caulking with papyrus or some other material may have become necessary as a boat aged and the seams began to let in water, the edge-joined planking, held tightly in place by close-set mortises, was normally sufficient to maintain a watertight hull.

The Khufu boat

The Khufu boat (fig. 66) provides us with an excellent example of the 'shell-first', edge-joined technique of boat building used by the Ancient Egyptians, and bears witness both to the skill of the shipwrights who built it and to the long tradition of boat building which preceded it.

Egyptologists had known of the existence of two sealed boat pits beside the Khufu pyramid for a long time, but it was only in the noon of 26 May 1954 that the dismantled parts of a large, wooden boat were finally brought into the light of day. When found, the boat was stacked in thirteen layers and comprised 1,224 pieces ranging from small dowels to

66 *Khufu's boat, with artist's impression of mast and rigging.*

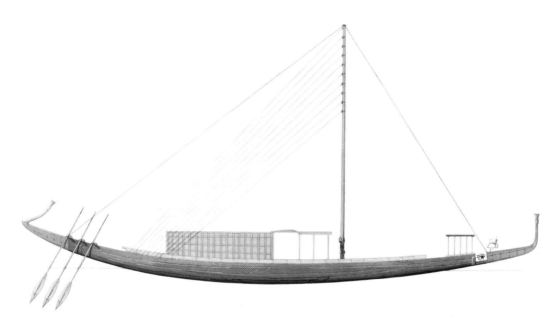

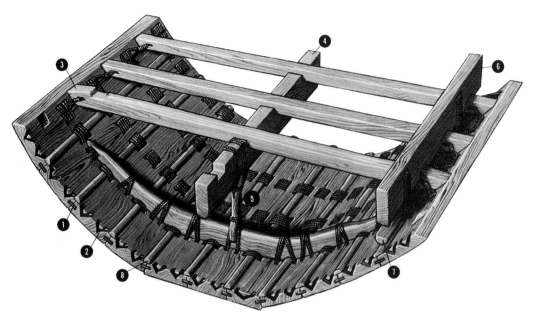

67 *Cross-section of planking on the Khufu boat.*

large timbers which once formed the topmost strakes on either side of the boat.

The keel-plank which forms the base of the whole structure is built up of segments made of eight short pieces of wood and was probably laid first. The planking of the hull was then built up to the required height on either side and bound together edge-to-edge with pegs (see fig. 67 (**1**)), and further consolidated by v-shaped stitching (**2**) which is invisible from the outside. The butt-ends of the planks are joined by s-shaped hook-scarves and long, narrow hemispherical battens are lashed over the seams to make them watertight (**8**). The shell of the boat is further strengthened by sixteen frames inserted in the hull bottom and lashed to the planking.

A long, central-shelf or stringer (**4**) runs down the middle of the boat supported at regular intervals on seven forked stanchions inserted into the frames at the bottom of the hull (**5**). This shelf supports forty-six cross-beams (**3**) inlet into the sides of the boat which, in turn, support the deck and the removable hatches laid over the cross-beams.

There is a large, rectangular deckhouse just aft of midships supported on side-girders at its base and on thirty-six columns with papyrus-bud finials along its sides (fig. 68). These columns support slender, curved beams which arch above the roof. The roof itself is supported internally on three columns with palm-shaped finials. The walls of the deckhouse consist of twelve wooden panels, five on each side, and one at each end. Access to the interior is gained through a double door secured from the inside by a sliding bolt. On the fore-deck is a small look-out or baldachin supported on ten slender, elegant poles with lotus-bud finials.

The boat has a displacement of 45 tons and is 43.4m long; 5.9m in the beam; and has a depth of 1.78m just aft of amidships. Its maximum draught is 1.48m.

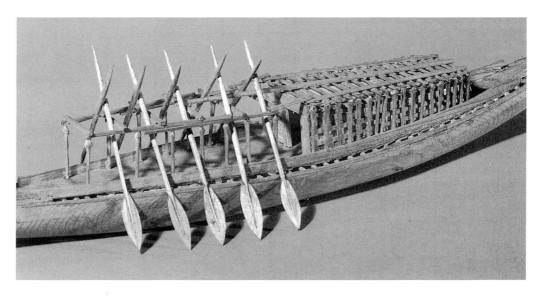

The vessel was originally propelled by five pairs of oars and steered by two steering-oars suspended over either quarter.

68 *Deck house from a model of the Khufu boat.*

The Dahshur boats

Further evidence of early boat building techniques was provided in 1894–5 by the discovery by the French archaeologist, Jean-Jacques de Morgan, of about six – the exact number is unresolved – hastily constructed boats buried in simple pits beside the pyramid of Senusret III at Dahshur. These may once have either formed part of the king's burial equipment or belonged to other members of the royal family (fig. 69). Today, two are located in the Cairo Museum, one at the Field Museum of Natural History at the University of Chicago, and another at the Carne-

69 *Dahshur boat of Senusret III.*

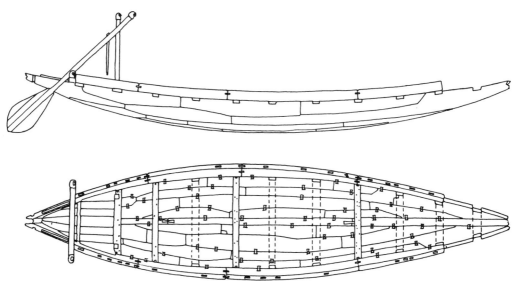

70 *Cross-section of the planking of the Dahshur boat showing dowels and butterfly-cramps.*

gie Museum in Pittsburgh. The exact whereabouts of the other two are unknown and it has been suggested that they may still be at Dahshur.

The vessels are round bottomed, broad in the beam and have gently curving sheers. All are of similar shape and size and their individual dimensions vary from 9.2 to 10.2m in length, 2.24 to 2.28m in width and 0.84 to 0.9m in depth. All display the same, traditional 'shell-first' method of construction as the Khufu boat.

In a recently published book, Cheryl Haldane has provided us with an excellent description of the boat at the Carnegie. It is built-up around a keel-plank composed of three sections of wood joined together with mortise-and-tenon joints measuring about 3cm deep and 3cm wide. The longest plank is 4.19m long, 1.2 m thick and 3.55 m wide at its maximum point. The strakes which form the sides of the vessel are made of short pieces of wood joined along their edges with mortise-and-tenon joints and shallow dovetail cramps inset into the wood from the inside. The gunwales are made up of sections lashed together at their ends and fastened to the uppermost strake by mortise-and-tenon joints.

Unlike the Khufu boat, there is no internal sewing and there are no strengthening frames inserted into the hull. Lateral strength is provided by several cross-beams which rest in notches cut in the upper edge of the topmost strake. These are fixed to the hull planking by dowels and secured by wooden pegs cut off flush with the outside of the hull. The thick planking and the framework of cross-beams are sufficient in themselves to create a stable hull and render frames unnecessary (fig. 70).

As was the custom, the hatches laid over the deck-beams were removable, allowing the boats to be adapted for different uses. Several of the cross-beams have v-shaped lashing holes in their surfaces which Haldane suggests may have been used to attach deck furnishings.

The bow and stern are cut off square, but they may once have had decorative finials since most have mortises at the bow. Although the hull-planking was originally held together by mortise-and-tenon and flat, dovetail cramps, most of these had disappeared at the time of the discovery.

Steering-oars, and the stanchions to support them, were buried with

the boats. When discovered, the decoration on the steering-oars and the posts on which they pivoted had for the most part disappeared, but the blue-wigged falcon heads which originally decorated the tops of the posts had survived on the pieces in Pittsburgh and Chicago. One boat also had small areas of white plaster on its hull, while one gunwale still preserved some remnants of the thin blue or black sheer-lines enclosed within one or two thicker red lines which once decorated it – a design peculiar to funerary boats.

71 Boats moored at the jetty at the city of Akhetaten, el-Amarna.

Haldane suggests that, in view of the shallowness of the butterfly cramps holding the shell of the hull together, the vessels may never in fact have been used on the river, but have functioned only as very large models!

DOCKYARDS/HARBOURS

Very little evidence has survived of the artificial harbours and dockyard workshops which must once have existed to accommodate and repair the large number of boats which sailed up and down the Nile. The earliest mention of a dockyard occurs on a seal of Queen Nimaathap from the reign of Peribsen of the Second Dynasty, which mentions a 'sealer of the dockyard workshop', while the first representation of a private dockyard occurs in the tomb of Rahotep of the Fourth Dynasty at Meidum. The importance of such installations is attested much later by a painting in the Sixth Dynasty mastaba of Kaemankh at Giza, which mentions a dockyard/workshop and depicts the different types of boats manufactured there, together with the tools used to construct them.

Although there can be little doubt that in the majority of cases the Ancient Egyptians either dragged their boats up on to the river bank or tied up fore and aft to mooring stakes, larger craft must have had more elaborate installations to accommodate them. Our only example of a jetty projecting from a bank comes from a tomb at Amarna, dating to the reign of Akhenaten (1353–1335 BC) (fig. 71). However, the titles of various individuals buried at Giza and Saqqara show that dockyards must have existed in the area from an early date. Nakht-zaes of the Fifth Dynasty and Ni-iuf-Ptah of the Sixth Dynasty held the title of 'Carpenter of the great dockyard', while another individual named Seshem-nefer

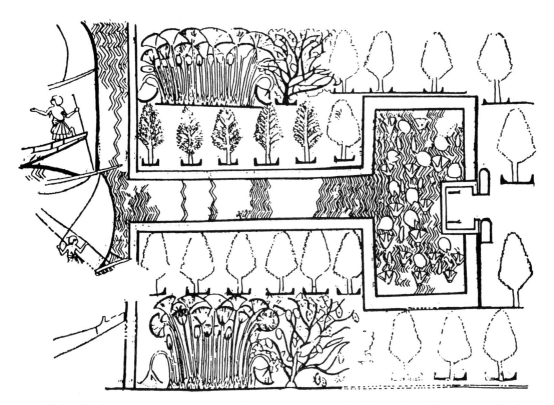

72 *T-shaped harbour before the temple of Amun-Ra at Karnak.*

was 'Carpenter of the great dockyard of the palace'. It appears that by Tuthmose III's (1479–1425 BC) and Amenhotep II's (1427–1401 BC) time, a settlement had grown up around the yards called 'Perunefer' or 'Good Departure' equipped with shipyards, temples and guest-houses for the reception of foreign envoys. The same dockyards continued to flourish during the Nineteenth Dynasty. Accounts from the reign of Sety I (1306–1290 BC) mention 'the dock of the charioteer Heri-nefer' situated south of Memphis as well as an 'Inspector of the dockyards', and Papyrus Lansing of the Twentieth Dynasty refers to the hardships endured by the shipwrights who worked there.

Although little evidence has survived of the harbours which served the provincial towns and cities, several depictions of temple harbours come from the Eighteenth and Nineteenth Dynasties. These stood in front of temples and consisted of rectangular basins with quays which were linked to the Nile by a canal. They were used not only to accommodate the temples' large fleets of cargo boats, but also as mooring places for the large ceremonial barges, such as the *Userhat*, which were used to transport the portable barks of gods from one location to another during religious festivals. Just such a T-shaped harbour, linked to the Nile by a canal, is depicted in the tomb of Neferhotep of the Eighteenth Dynasty. This was located before the Temple of Amun-Ra at Thebes during the reign of Amenhotep III (1391–1353 BC), (fig. 72). The stone landing-stage of a later quay built by Ramses II over that of Amenhotep III can still be seen today by visitors to Karnak. Other examples which once served the mortuary temples of Amenhotep I and Tuthmose III at Thebes are depicted in the tombs of Amenmose and Khons of the Nineteenth Dynasty, while excavation has revealed that similar harbours once existed at the royal palace of Amenhotep III at Malkata and the temple of Ramses III at Medinet Habu.

The existence of a stone landing quay called the 'Head-of-the-Canal' (*tep sha*, *tep en sha*) at the temple of Dendera in Upper Egypt would suggest that all the larger temples were similarly provided. A funerary papyrus in the British Museum mentions a certain Nebamun, the 'Overseer of the Dockyard of Amun in the Southern City' (that is, Thebes), who may well have had overall responsibility for the harbour and yards located there.

DOCKYARD AND PORT PERSONNEL

Although the evidence is sparse, it would be reasonable to assume that the most important towns possessed facilities for the construction and maintenance of boats and the harbours and dockyards which served them. These installations (*wekhryt, meryt, meniwt*) must have possessed governing bodies administered by such men as Kenamun at Perunefer near Memphis and Nebamun at Thebes, and a host of other officials whose work was related to trade and ship construction: the weighers who measured the grain stored in the granaries ready for distribution and scribes who kept records of such transactions; caulkers, sail- and rope-makers and the like; dock workers who unloaded the cargoes and stevedores who carried the merchandise to the storage areas. Several paintings clearly show boats with gang-planks set in place, while scenes of men unloading cargo would suggest the existence of port facilities and a busy waterborne trade in a variety of commodities.

Several passages attest to the existence of a well-organised bureaucracy in Egypt which ran the ports and policed the river traffic. An Eleventh Dynasty stela mentions the 'Overseer of all police patrols on water and on land' whose duty it was to regulate river traffic and, in sensitive areas, to act as immigration control officers. An inscription at Semna dating to the eighth year of Senusret III shows that the most stringent measures were taken to prevent foreigners from entering Egypt, by water or by land:

> ***Southern boundary made in year 8 ... to prevent any foreigner from passing it downstream or overland or by boat [also] any herds of foreigners, apart from any foreigner who shall come to trade at Iken or upon any good business that may be done with them. (BAR I, §293)***

The oldest reference to what may be a control-point (opinions differ) is to be found in the inscription of Djehutyhotep of the Middle Kingdom from Bersheh, which mentions 'the officials who were made [judges] in this city who were appointed to the control-point[?] on the river'.

A passage from an Act of Endowment of the Temple of Khons instructs officials:

> *...that their* [that is, the temples'] *ships be not stopped by any patrol; that their ships be not taken by [lawful] seizure in order to carry out the commissions of Pharaoh. (BAR IV, §147)*

The Nauri and fragmentary Elephantine decrees of Sety I (1306–1290 BC) and Ramses III (1194–1163 BC) forbid any police patrol from detaining ships of the temple estates. The latter king also 'appointed slaves as watchmen of your [the Temple of Karnak] harbour, in order to watch the harbour of the Helipolitan canal' (BAR IV, §266). Some time later, a demotic document, dating to the reign of Darius, informs us that, under Psamtek I (c. 664–610 BC), a certain Padiaset and his son Smatutefnakht were 'Masters of the harbours or shipping' of Herakleopolis.

The same king also placed restrictions on Greek trading with Egypt. Greek ships were required to sail up the Canopic branch of the Nile and discharge their cargoes at the newly established trading post of Naucratis in the western delta (Herodotus, *Histories* II, §154).

Conclusion

In the Old Kingdom boats were flat bottomed and square ended with broad, shallow hulls stiffened internally by the insertion of frames and cross-beams and by the addition of girt-ropes and trusses when sea voyages or a more demanding role were intended. The stern was generally higher than the prow, which was either square ended or carved into the shape of an animal head.

They were equipped with a tall, oblong sail, narrower at the base than at the head, which was suspended on a bipod or straddle mast, stepped well forward. Despite their height, however, they could be unstepped when not in use, and supported either on forked crutches or lowered on to a gantry at the stern, so that they would not endanger the vessel's trim.

On primitive papyrus craft, the sail was perhaps originally made of papyrus matting but this was soon replaced by linen which was far more durable. It was secured to a fixed lower yard which rested on the deck and was hoisted on a upper yard. The mast was securely stayed with a back-stay and shrouds which are conventionally depicted abaft the mast. A fore-stay was later introduced. When the sail was lowered, the vessel was propelled by a crew of rowers who faced aft or by paddlers who faced forward.

A simple awning or plaited matting supported on a wooden framework of cross-poles and supporting columns, located abaft the mast, provided shelter for the crew. Larger shelters extended almost the whole length of the deck.

In the early part of the Old Kingdom, boats were steered by several hand-held oars on each quarter, but by the late Sixth Dynasty it had become customary to lash the loom of the steering-oar to a vertical stanchion, a system which continued in use down to the end of the dynastic period. A tiller was introduced some time in the Fifth Dynasty to help control the movement of the steering-oar.

From the late Old Kingdom Egyptian shipwrights began to build boats whose hulls were round bottomed and spoon shaped. As before, they were beamy and drew little water.

After the close of the Old Kingdom the pole mast gradually became the principal method of suspending the sail. Although stepped in the same way, it was not as high as before and was located closer to the mid-line of the vessel. From the same time the sail was bent to a yard which, because of its increased length, was normally made of two spars lashed together at mid-point. The boom or lower yard was held against the mast by a parrel-lashing which allowed it to turn freely on its axis.

With the introduction of the broader sail from the beginning of the Sixth Dynasty a different method of suspending the sail had to be found. At first the boom rested directly upon the deck and did not need any support. However, with the introduction of a broader sail which was carried higher above deck, the lower and upper yards had to be supported by ropes, called lifts. These ran between the yards and the mast-head and were attached to a calcet or to a series of protruding rings on either side of the mast, usually situated immediately below the halyard-block.

After the Old Kingdom the steering gear consisted of a single, large oar suspended over the stern or later, in the New Kingdom, in a longitudinal recess in the extreme stern of the vessel. The introduction of this fixed type of steering gear led to a reduction in the number of helmsmen from around five in the Old Kingdom to one or two in the Middle and New Kingdoms.

Different types of boats had also emerged to meet different needs: pilgrimage boats, harem boats and escort boats to protect the nomarchs in the times of civil unrest at the close of the Old Kingdom.

Boats of the New Kingdom, and thereafter, preserve the same general features as their Middle Kingdom predecessors and such differences as exist are confined to their size and variety. The hull retains its well-rounded form. Cross-beams protrude through the side of the planking to give extra rigidity to the hull and a much improved system of rope-truss was introduced on sea-going ships. The deckhouse was enlarged and now occupied the central portion of the ship and, on large ships, the mast had become fixed. Sails were rigged much lower on the mast and the yards which carried them were often as long as the vessels themselves. Ornate lookouts and kiosks were built on deck and many of the ships were elaborately decorated. The steering-gear remained substantially the same as in the Middle Kingdom although extra rope-tackles were added to give it additional stability. The mast-head fixture which supported the standing and running rigging was also improved and a rack on the deck abaft the mast was added to secure the halyards.

Despite the paucity of evidence, there appears to be little change in the basic shape and design of Ancient Egyptian ships after the close of the

New Kingdom. Ramses III's warships certainly display novel features (the so-called 'ram' in the bows, the fighting top at the mast-head and the loose-footed sail), but one is ill equipped to gauge the lasting influence such innovations had on the mainstream tradition of shipbuilding in Egypt. Perhaps the only significant naval event which occurred during the Pharaonic period was the introduction of Greek triremes by Nekau in the Twenty-Sixth Dynasty, but one suspects that these may have been little more than an alien graft – controlled as they were by Greek mercenaries – on an otherwise resilient Egyptian boat-building tradition. The papyri mention 'Greek boats' on the Nile, but the most common, the *baris*, was still constructed in the traditional Egyptian way. Herodotus' testimony also indicates that the more time-honoured method of boat building was still very much alive and well in his day – at least on freighters – and, even in more recent times, the Nilotic *naggr* (*nuggar*) still preserved many of the features of its pharaonic predecessors.

Glossary of terms

Abaft	behind, on the stern side of.
After-deck	short raised deck on a platform at the stern.
Amidships	in the middle of the vessel.
Back-stay	a rope used to brace the mast against oblique pressures and usually secured to the stern or later to a rack inset into the main deck in front of the steering-oar posts.
Beam	extreme width of a vessel.
Bend	to fix the sail to *yards* ready for hoisting.
Boom	the lower *yard* to which is fitted the foot of the sail.
Bow	forward end of the vessel.
Bowlines	rarely shown. These lines run from the leading edge of the sail to a point forward to keep the *leech* flat when the ship was sailing on the wind.
Braces	ropes attached to upper *yards* used to trim the sail at a suitable angle to the wind.
Brails	lines for shortening a *loose-footed* sail. Brails were made fast to the foot, travelled up the forward surface through fairleads sewn in vertical rows, passed over the yard and came down to the aft deck.
Break	the sudden rise or fall of the deck when not flush.
Bulwark	the part of the hull which frames the deck.
Butt of oar	upper or handle end.
Carvel-build	vessel whose hull planks are laid flush edge to edge.
Caulk	to insert material into the seams of the deck or planking to make the junction watertight.
Central-shelf	a narrow longitudinal timber running down the middle of the vessel from *stem* to *stern* at deck level.
Clinker-build	a method of boat building in which the lower edge of each side plank overlaps the upper edge of the one below it. Also known as 'lapstrake'.
Comb	semicircular flanges or rings fixed immediately below the *halyard*-block on either side of the mast to which the lifts of the lower *yard* or *boom* are fixed.
Cringles	a short piece of rope worked *grommet* fashion into the bolt-rope of a sail.
Cross-beam/	horizontal timbers running from side-to-side of the

thwarts	vessel that support the deck and give lateral rigidity to the hull.
Deck	a platform of planks extending from side to side of the vessel or part of it.
Finials	the wooden extensions fitted to the stem and stern of a vessel.
Fore-deck	a short, raised deck or platform at the bow.
Fore-stay	rope running from the mast-head and secured to the *bow* to support the mast.
Furl	the operation of taking in the sail and securing it with *gaskets*.
Gantry	a raised wooden frame consisting of two upright posts joined by a cross-piece on which the mast could be rested when unstepped.
Gasket	a rope, plaited cord, or strip of canvas used to secure a sail when furled to a *yard* or *boom*.
Girdle-truss	the rope that encircled the boat just below the *gunwales*.
Girt-rope	the rope that encircled the prow and stern of the boat to which the *hogging-truss* was attached.
Grommet	a strand of rope laid up in the form of a ring. One of its uses was to hold the oars to the *thole-pins* when rowing.
Gunwale	the upper edge of the *bulwark* (line of planks above the deck-line on the side of boat).
Halyard-block	the block immediately below the mast-head, pierced with holes to take the *halyards* of the sail and the middle topping-lifts of the upper yard. Sometimes referred to as the 'calcet'.
Halyards	ropes used to hoist or lower sail.
Hogging-truss	a heavy rope under tension secured around the hull at the stem and stern and supported on one or more stanchions above deck level. It provided longitudinal rigidity to the hull in the absence of a keel.
Keel	the lowest and principal timber of a wooden ship on which the framework (*ribs* and planking) of the whole is built up.
Larboard	the left-hand side of the vessel looking forward. Later also known as 'port' side.
Leeches	the edges of the sail.